FORM

& FOLIAGE GUIDE TO

PLANTING

FORM

& FOLIAGE GUIDE TO

PLANTING

Jennifer Stackhouse & Helen Young

MURDOCH
B O O K S

CONTENTS

There's no denying that the flowers on a plant enhance its beauty. Pick up any book on plants and you'll find that much of the information centres around the flowering aspect of plants. There are detailed descriptions on the type of bloom, their myriad colours, heady perfumes and flowering seasons. The same thing applies to most labels on plants— the emphasis is on the plants' flowering potential. But, as you'll discover, plants have a lot more to offer than just their flowers. And, when it comes to looking at plants as elements in garden design, flowers are transient details.

No matter how gorgeous the flowers, their impact lasts only for a few weeks or perhaps months. Next time you choose a garden plant, don't be seduced by its bloom alone. Instead, ask yourself how this particular plant will look for the rest of the year, when it is not in flower but is still taking up precious garden space.

As garden sizes shrink and time, too, is at a premium, the plants we grow have to perform. Unless you're an ardent collector, there's no room, or time, in most gardens for one-day wonders. Plants that give year-round

Once a cottage garden was home to useful plants that included herbs, fruits and vegetables. Today, it's simply a happy blending of all types of plants. Previous pages: Massed daisies and watsonias in soft pastel shades.

interest are particularly important for small gardens, courtyards or in areas where plants are grown in containers. Plant structure becomes increasingly significant as more emphasis is given to enjoying gardens as living pictures viewed from indoors, framed through a door or window. And with the recent developments in garden lighting, plants can be on show at night as well as by day. Under lights, plant form and structure become all important while flowers and even foliage take a back seat.

Most plants offer much more than seasonal blooms. Indeed, there's an entire framework of vegetation and growth that the plant produces just to support its flowers from bud to seed. Plants are made up of leaves, stems, branches and roots. These features are arranged so each individual plant has a distinctive and characteristic look. Some species are particularly captivating, so much so that they become more than just plants growing in the soil, they become living sculptures.

In this book we've gathered together a selection of plants that are distinctive because of the arrangement of their stems and leaves. Our focus is on the overall form of plants and on the colour, shape and texture of

Opposite: Plan your garden so it creates interest all year round. A simple combination of evergreen trees and shrubs, colourful perennials and bold, lush ferns give this garden pleasing form and a sense of harmony.

their foliage. We don't ignore flowers or fruit, but consider them a bonus rather than the main reason to grow a plant.

The key, then, to having a great-looking garden that has interest all year round is to choose plants that have both form and foliage. This doesn't mean that transient plants should be completely ignored. Some short-lived plants do have a fascinating shape and form that warrants their inclusion in the framework of the garden. Indeed, bulbs and herbaceous perennials, particularly the ornamental grasses, provide an eye-catching structure, even if the display lasts for only a couple of months. For this reason, we have included some of the more impressive grasses.

All the plants featured in this book have good structure and long-lasting garden interest. Our choices have been based on overall shape as well as leaf colour, texture and shape. These plants make a statement, either singly as a dramatic focal point, or massed together as solid shapes or blocks of texture. There is wide variety in the plant forms, ranging from compact rosettes (including many of the succulents) to spreading carpet-like species such as ajuga and dianthus. We've also listed plants that offer lush and

The striking form and fiery colours of the red-hot poker provide a dramatic backdrop for a clump of feathery *Perovskia* with its tiny, mauve flowers. Following pages: Luxuriant foliage and a pond create a tranquil oasis.

often colourful foliage, just the thing for creating a jungle or tropical look. And there are others that make a dramatic impact. These bold and vibrant plants can give a garden an instant 'wow! factor'.

We look at plants that form clumps with both strappy and spiky choices and examine species that grow naturally into pleasing shapes such as buns, cones and balls. And there are others that can be clipped into shape.

We also discuss ways to use plants effectively in garden design. For example, clumping plants with strappy leaves, such as agapanthus, clivias and narcissus, take on a formal role when they are arranged in rows or blocks, giving uniformity and direction to a garden. But these plants can acquire an informal air when they're planted in random groups.

By contrast, spiky plants make an exclamation point in a garden. They have a crisp, pointed outline that makes them an ideal choice as a living sculpture or as the plant to use when a certain sharpness is required. When mass-planted, they contribute an exciting, active texture.

There is a host of ideas for creating rich variety and contrast in the garden. For example, select a bold, lush foliage plant then accentuate its

Random plantings of mixed foliage, flowers and succulents create rich variety, texture and contrast; the splashes of colour add to the appeal.

shape by partnering it with a sharp, spiky clump. Spiky plants also contrast well with strappy clumps or with plants that naturally form a ball shape. And don't overlook the power of carpet plants. We show how these plants are used to soften hard edges in the landscape, such as steps, stairs and pathways, or as an underplanting beneath a single dramatic spire.

Good planting techniques are the basis of a successful garden. There is no greater disappointment than when carefully selected plants fail to thrive, or their growth or shape fails to live up to your expectations. For this reason, we've included basic details on each plant—height, spread, flowering season—as well as growing requirements.

The major factors that affect the success or failure of a garden plant are the nature of the soil and the amount of sun, water and food it receives. Extreme temperatures—either very hot or very cold—along with strong winds and salt air can also take their toll on a plant's health and vigour. To get good growth, it is essential to match the plant to the climatic conditions in your area and specifically, in your garden.

If you live in a cold or frost-prone area, avoid plants that hate the cold unless you can grow them indoors or in a conservatory. If you spot the

Contrasting foliage plants, such as tree ferns, elephant's ears and strappy grasses, overlap the boardwalk, giving this water garden a luxuriant feel.

words 'frost tender' in a plant description, don't choose it for your garden. Heat intolerance can also be a problem. If you live in a hot climate, skip plants that are recommended for cool to mild climates—they'll just bring you heartache. The correct choice for sun and shade is just as vital. Plants that love the sun need lots of it to grow well. If your garden is shaded, avoid sun-loving plants—be assured, there are lots of wonderful shade-loving plants to enjoy in a shady garden. And conversely, don't plant shade-loving plants in open spaces where they'll be burnt by a blazing sun.

Soil and planting methods play major roles in garden success. Most of the plants featured in this book like soils that are rich and well drained. This means the soil has lots of nutrients with which to feed the plant. The soil also absorbs water, then allows it to flow through the root system and drain away. Soils that are poorly drained are usually clay-based and can form wells that hold water rather than allowing it to drain away. The result is a root system that can't grow properly and may be affected by disease.

There are also soils with the opposite problem: they drain too freely or fail to let water soak in. These are usually sandy soils and are sometimes

Pruned and trained into a contorted shape, this pittosporum gives strong contrast to the luxuriant profusion of the rest of the garden.
Following pages: The sun-drenched, but moist, edges of a pond are ideal for sweeps of water iris and bold clumps of gunnera.

known as hydrophobic (water repellent). The best soil falls between the two types and is known as loam. Don't worry if your soil doesn't meet optimum requirements. Most soils can be cultivated and enriched with nutrients by adding organic matter such as well-rotted manure and compost.

If the drainage in your garden is sluggish, conditions can be improved by digging in gypsum or by creating raised planting beds that will hold plant roots above the slow-draining soil. Where soils are hard to wet, or simply dry out too quickly, add wetting agents or water-absorbent crystals and moisture-holding materials such as organic matter. This will also improve growth because these materials trap the moisture in the soil long enough to be of benefit to the plant.

Even where growing conditions are spot on, many plants still fail. This is often because they were planted incorrectly in the first place. While a plant's root system is below ground level, it still needs air. These air pockets do not have to be big, but simply tiny pores that form naturally between the soil particles. If a plant's roots are buried deeply in the soil they can be robbed of air and will fail to grow.

Garden ornaments, such as pots, urns, fountains and statuary, bring another dimension to the landscape. They can give a garden character, structure and interesting form and most pieces have the advantage of being mobile.

When digging a hole for a new plant, make it as deep as the container the plant is in, but no deeper. As you take the plant out of its container, look at the point at which the stem emerges from the potting mix. The top of the soil in the pot, from where the stem emerges, should still be visible at the surface of the garden bed after it is planted. This ensures that the rootball has not been buried by extra soil.

To keep the right balance between air and moisture, firm the plant into position using your hands and water. Don't trample around a newly planted tree or shrub with your feet—that's a sure way of causing damage. Instead, let water from a hose or a watering can percolate through the soil, removing large air spaces and helping the roots to settle into the right position. If the soil slumps down, add more soil but don't bury the stem.

Finally, cover the soil surface around the plant with a layer of organic mulch. Spread 5–7 cm (2–3 inches) of mulch, taking care not to build it up around the stem. Regular watering while the new roots are developing and an occasional dose of appropriate plant food as growth appears, should be sufficient to get a plant off to a great start.

A rich tapestry of contrasting foliage plants makes a dynamic statement.

The plants featured in this book are grouped according to their shape and foliage interest. Then, within each chapter, they are arranged alphabetically by their botanical name. Common names are also included.

Each chapter details the design potential and planting information for a particular group of plants. At the end of each chapter there is a special section that provides extra information on the group of plants discussed in the chapter. In Dramatic, the special section focuses on plants that produce tall flower spires. Potted collections are highlighted in Rosettes and the versatile cactus hits the spotlight in Spiky. If you like plants with interesting shapes or would like to know how it's done, Topiary in the Shapes and Hedges chapter is sure to inspire. The wonderful palm, in all its many forms, is detailed in Lush and Coloured, while ornamental grasses get the attention in Strappy. In Carpets, the focus is on soft plants that are used to soften the edges of pathways, walls and fences.

Although extensive, our selection of plants is by no means definitive—there just isn't the room! But we hope that our selections, many of them our favourites, will inspire you to explore the world of form and foliage in your garden and to see plants with new eyes.

Rhapis palms and dense foliage plants create a lush and tropical garden. There are tropical-style plants that are suitable for cold climates, too.

DRAMATIC

Like your garden to have the wow! factor? All it takes is a couple of strategically placed, drop-dead-gorgeous plants and you bring instant drama to the garden. Dramatic plants are nature's show ponies, the ones that stand out from the crowd. They can be wildy flamboyant, colourful, unusually shaped, larger than life and strikingly beautiful. Their exciting credentials mean they

Few plants are as sculptural as the Australian grass tree, *Xanthorrhoea* species, whether in the bush or in a garden. Previous pages: The colourful spires of Russell lupins are bold and dramatic, especially in a cool-climate garden.

have huge pulling power, making an ordinary garden spectacular.

Dramatic plants are best used where they will have the biggest impact—as a single specimen, mass-planted, lining a fence or pathway, potted and placed on either side of a doorway or positioned where they're least expected to create an element of surprise. The following selection of dramatic plants will inspire you.

The flower clusters of the spear lily (*Doryanthes excelsa*) (left) sit atop long stems, 3 metres (8 ft) or more high. Closer to earth are cottagey foxgloves and lupins (right). Following pages: Crotons, sansevieria and cane palms.

ALOE SPECIES
ALOE

The leaves of A. *marlothii* are sharply serrated and topped by bold spires of burnt-orange flowers. These vibrant blooms, usually seen in winter and early spring, provide nectar for birds.

For variety and spectacle, aloes are hard to beat. Most of the 300-strong species have large, succulent (sometimes prickly) leaves in an interesting array of sizes, shapes and colours. Brightly coloured flowers appear on spires or candelabras in shades of red, orange, yellow and, occasionally, lime-green. Many aloes flower in winter or early spring, adding drama at a time when other plants may have closed down. The aloe in flower is a show in itself—but wait until the birds start their feeding frenzy on the nectar-filled flowers.

Some aloes hug the ground. Others, like *Aloe arborescens*, become tree-like with a tall trunk and branching arms. These can grow 2–3 metres (6–10 ft) tall. Many aloes have fascinating forms: *A. polyphylla* has its leaves arranged in an elegant spiral pattern, while *A. plicatilis* has fans of leaves on stout, knobbly stems up to 1.5 metres (5 ft) tall. And one of the smallest aloes, *A. aristata*, at 10 cm (4 inches) tall, forms a dense rosette of lance-shaped, toothed, dark-green leaves speckled in white.

One of the handiest aloes is *A. vera*, which has medicinal properties; it is used widely for treating burns. Simply break open a leaf and apply the cool sap directly onto a burn.

Aloe vera can grow happily in a pot. Opposite: Consider the outline of foliage against the sky when planting for dramatic results as shown by this aloe.

GROWING NOTES

The large species of aloe enjoy full sun and well-drained soil. Some of their smaller relatives are tolerant of shade. Most aloes have sharply pointed, spiky leaves so they should be placed where they can be seen but not touched. The stems and lower leaves often become unkempt so, from time to time, tidy them up by removing dead leaves and spent flower stalks.

Aloes are very easy to propagate. Most produce offsets around the main plant that can simply be detached and planted into the ground or a pot of free-draining potting mix. Alternatively, they can be struck readily from a stem cutting. Aloes thrive in heat and drought and many tolerate light frost but, in cold-winter areas, they need protection from the cold.

BISMARCKIA NOBILIS
BISMARCK PALM

It originates from Madagascar, but it was 19th-century German botanists who named *Bismarckia* in honour of Germany's first chancellor, Otto von Bismarck, who was commonly known as the 'Iron Chancellor'.

The Bismarck palm is nothing short of spectacular. It has a crown of stiff, silver-blue leaves that form masses of wonderful fan shapes. The overall effect is surreal, resembling a spiky, metallic puffball. This striking Madagascan native also has a green form but it lacks the 'oomph' factor of its spacey, silvery-blue cousin. The Bismarck palm makes a great stand-alone feature, the perfect living sculpture. Its metallic-like sheen also contrasts beautifully with green foliage plants, especially those with similar-shaped leaves. In its natural habitat, this palm can grow 60 metres (120 ft) high, but is much smaller in gardens. Its large, lance-shaped leaves are around 2–3 metres (6–10 ft) long. Young plants can be raised in containers, but it's probably best to position this relatively fast-growing plant with its feet firmly in the ground.

GROWING NOTES
The Bismarck palm prefers the tropics to subtropics but will grow in temperate and inland zones with frost protection. It prefers an open site with sandy, well-drained soil. It tolerates drought and is suitable for an arid or dry, tropical landscape.

DICKSONIA ANTARCTICA
SOFT TREE FERN

Of all the ferns, *Dicksonia antarctica*, with its large, graceful fronds and furry trunk, is the most recognizable and dramatic. This native of southern Australia can be used to bring height to a fern garden or as an exotic touch in a cool, shaded area. Plants can reach to around 2–3 metres (6–10 ft) tall with a spread of up to 3 metres (10 ft), so give them plenty of space for spreading. They can grow tall enough to walk under, giving a delightful rainforest feel.

GROWING NOTES

The soft tree fern prefers shaded, moist and sheltered conditions. New fronds unfurl from the centre of the crown, which must be kept moist. Water plants from above using a sprinkler, or by positioning an irrigation micro-spray head among the fronds. Plants are often sold as cut trunks, which will take hold when they're replanted. The brown 'dust' that issues from the fern, or is seen in felty patches on the back of the fronds, is not the sign of a sick plant. It is, in fact, millions of tiny spores necessary for reproduction.

Above: Soft tree ferns like a cool, sheltered spot.
Opposite: There are many different tree ferns and all need space in which to spread their fronds.

DORYANTHES EXCELSA
GYMEA LILY, SPEAR LILY

As a clump of green, sword-like leaves *Doryanthes excelsa* is very much the attention-grabber, but the drama doesn't stop there. Slowly, over many months, a stout, straight flower stalk appears, looking like an oversized asparagus spear. The flowers, which normally open in spring, develop on top of this huge stem, which can grow 6 metres (20 ft) tall. The buds open to reveal a cluster of red lilies that are attractive to birds. These blooms are also much sought after for floral work. Flowers last for several months and may form seeds.

GROWING NOTES

In their natural, temperate to subtropical habitat gymea lilies grow in open but sheltered areas, often under trees. They tolerate filtered shade and will grow in full sun if they are kept well watered. Plants need a well-drained soil that's rich in organic matter. Water well as the flower stalk forms. To keep plants looking good, prune the spent stem once the show is over (unless seeds are needed for propagation).

The leaves of the gymea lily measure 2–2.5 metres (6–8 ft) in length, but it's the tall flower spike that steals the show.

DRACAENA DRACO
DRAGON'S BLOOD TREE

Set the dragon's blood tree against a plain backdrop to highlight its fascinating form. With age, the tree becomes broad, spreading and gnarled.

The dragon's blood tree oozes drama—both in its unique form and its intriguing common name. It has a short, stout trunk that branches into a broad, umbrella-shaped canopy, with crowns of blue-green rosettes growing from thick, upswept branches. The summer flowers are barely noticeable, but the orange berries that follow stand out among the leaves. Grow this tree as a free-standing specimen in a lawn or garden, or use it as a feature in a huge container. It is very slow growing, but with age the trunk will reach 7–9 metres (25–30 ft) tall and can be 1 metre (3 ft) in diameter. And the name? It comes from the blood-red colour of its sap.

GROWING NOTES

The dragon's blood tree can be grown in any frost-free tropical to temperate garden in full sun. Give it lots of room to spread out and form its broad canopy up to 18 metres (60 ft) across. Once established, it is drought hardy. This tree is a native of the Canary Islands, making it ideal for coastal areas.

ECHIUM SPECIES
PRIDE OF MADEIRA

Delightful echiums add their special brand of drama to the garden in a warm and fuzzy way. These pretty plants have tall, dense flower spikes in glorious shades and rosettes of furry leaves. En masse, they are breathtakingly beautiful. The pride of Madeira (*Echium candicans* syn. *E. fastuosum*) is the best known of all. It has brilliant bluish-purple flower spires that stand 60 cm (2 ft) above the foliage. The plant grows as a long-lived shrub and may sprawl to form a large clump of more than 2 metres (6 ft) in width. The furry, grey-green leaves accentuate the intense blue of the flowers. Also dramatic is the red *E. wildpretii*, which takes two years to flower. It's well worth the wait as the spires can grow to 1.8 metres (6 ft) tall.

GROWING NOTES

Echium prefers a well-drained soil, full sun and an open site. Plants do best in a Mediterranean climate or near the coast, but will tolerate any temperate climate if given an airy spot. Prune after flowering and, from time to time, remove old plants to make way for new ones. Plants self-seed in temperate climates.

The richly coloured flowers of the pride of Madeira are long-lasting and make an impact in a sunny garden.

GUNNERA MANICATA
GUNNERA, GIANT RHUBARB

The surreal gunnera must be seen to be believed. It has huge leaves (some of which are the largest of the broad-leafed plants) and green or red-brown flower spikes. The prickle-edged leaves quickly unfold in spring, growing to a width of 1–2.5 metres (3–8 ft) by summer. The stalks, which are also prickly, can grow 1.8 metres (6 ft) high. Gunnera thrives in boggy soil and makes a dramatic feature planting around a lake or pond. Contrast the huge, round leaves of gunnera with upright spiky plants, or enjoy their reflection in a water feature. Although quickly hidden by the spreading leaves, the summer flower spikes also make a dramatic impact.

In spring the new leaves and flower spikes appear from bare ground. By early summer, the leaves are gigantic, creating a canopy over the flowers.

GROWING NOTES

Gunnera does best in a cool to mild climate in moist soil that's rich in organic matter. It tolerates full sun to part shade. Cut plants back in autumn to remove spent foliage. Plants become dormant in winter, but in cold, frosty climates they need thick mulch around their roots for winter protection.

HELIANTHUS ANNUUS
SUNFLOWER

Not all sunflowers are yellow. This 'Russian Giant' (above) has bold bronze-coloured flowers. Larger than life, the golden sunflower is a garden treasure.

Bright and cheery sunflowers are fast growers that offer rich golden colour throughout the summer months. These tall-stemmed beauties have large, daisy-like, yellow flower heads with round brown centres. Massed or planted along a fence they bring instant drama and character to the garden. Sunflowers can reach 3 metres (10 ft) in height and can be too large for some gardens. However, there are smaller forms that grow to a more compact 1–1.5 metres (3–5 ft), such as the cute, double-flowered 'Teddy Bear' and 'Autumn Beauty', which comes in shades of red, brown, light yellow and golden yellow.

GROWING NOTES
Sunflowers need full sun and protection from strong winds to prevent damage, particularly to tall growers. They need to be well nourished, so dig plenty of organic matter into the soil before sowing the seeds. Space seeds 50–60 cm (20–24 inches) apart—thin the clumps to leave one strong seedling. Fertilize in spring to promote large blooms, and water well.

LICUALA SPECIES
FAN PALM

The fan palm is big on presentation and makes a dramatic impact in a warm-climate garden. It has rich textural appeal with its large, pleated, fan-shaped or circular leaves that are toothed around the perimeter. They come in various shades of green. Flowers are white or yellowish followed by red or brown berries. Several species are suited to gardens, including *Licuala grandis*, with its glossy, green leaves up to 1 metre (3 ft) across, and *L. ramsayi*, a native Australian species with a slender trunk, topped by a crown of magnificent circular leaves. The fan palm can grow from 6–20 metres (18–60 ft) tall. Position the plant where it will catch the light, to highlight the shape and form of its exciting foliage.

GROWING NOTES
The fan palm best suits tropical and subtropical gardens but will tolerate a warm, frost-free temperate climate where there's protection from wind and cold. This slow-growing palm prefers partial shade and sandy, well-drained soil. It can be grown in large containers outdoors or, in cooler areas, in a conservatory. Grow fan palms in a sheltered spot, especially when young and keep their soil moist and well mulched with organic matter.

The pleated, fan-shaped leaves of *Licuala grandis* can grow to 1 metre (3 ft) in diameter. These magnificent fronds are easily damaged by wind so grow this palm in a sheltered spot.

NELUMBO NUCIFERA

SACRED LOTUS

The flower of the sacred lotus features a distinctive golden boss that dries to form a pepper-pot-shaped seed head. Unlike the waterlily, both the flowers and leaves of *Nelumbo nucifera* rise above the surface of the water.

With its handsome, almost circular, leaves and its showy flower, the sacred lotus is an ideal specimen plant for a pond in a tropical garden. The leaves are visually exciting, rising above the water, and growing to 1 metre (3 ft) wide. The white or pink flowers are exotic in both shape and perfume. Enjoy these many-petalled blooms on long stalks from spring to late summer. Even the pepper-pot-shaped seed heads that follow deserve attention and are often used dried in flower arrangements or as ornaments.

If you do not have a water feature, don't dismiss the sacred lotus. Despite its size, it doesn't need deep water, especially in cooler climates. A single plant will happily grow in a large, water-filled container. In ponds, the sacred lotus will need 60–250 cm (2–8 ft) of water.

GROWING NOTES

The sacred lotus prefers an open, sunny position in tropical and subtropical areas. In cooler areas it can be grown in an indoor pond or large container. This plant grows from circular roots that give rise to both leaves and flowers. It can be planted in spring directly into the base of the pond or grown in submerged baskets or pots. It will not tolerate extremely cold conditions in winter. Check for frost hardiness when purchasing plants as some tropical forms are frost tender.

The solitary, fragrant blooms of the sacred lotus, in a range of gorgeous colours, are borne on long stalks.

PHYLLOSTACHYS NIGRA
BLACK BAMBOO

Bamboo is bold, fast growing and dramatic, but it can be an absolute pest—it all depends on how it is grown. The two types of bamboo are running (which need control) and clumping (which don't get out of hand). As a clump contained in a large pot or escape-proof garden bed, bamboo is hard to beat as a hedge, screen or living sculpture. Uncontrolled, running bamboo is invasive and a recognized weed. Many desirable species, including black bamboo, have coloured and patterned stems to about 6 metres (20 ft) tall. Accentuate stem colours by removing the lower leaves and positioning plants against a wall. A bonus is the pleasant rustling sound of the bamboo leaves when they're blown by the wind.

The tall, black stems of *Phyllostachys nigra* have been stripped of their lower leaves to create a strong, vertical accent. Opposite: Here the leaves provide vivid contrast to the bright red background.

GROWING NOTES

It's most important that bamboo is contained, particularly the running types. Most bamboos grow well in containers but do demand frequent watering, especially in hot or windy conditions. In the ground, control invasive runners by sinking a barrier into the ground to a depth of at least 1 metre (3 ft). Bamboo tolerates sun or shade and grows best in well-drained soil enriched with organic matter.

PLATYCERIUM SPECIES

STAGHORN AND ELKHORN FERNS

Staghorn (*Platycerium superbum*) and elkhorn (*P. bifurcatum*) ferns make wonderful living garden ornaments. These lush plants perch among tree branches in tropical and subtropical rainforests, producing cascades of foliage as they grow. They can transform a shady garden into a tropical oasis and create interest in a courtyard. As staghorn and elkhorn ferns are epiphytic, they don't need to be grown in soil. Instead, they can be nestled in a rock crevice, or mounted on a wall or tree trunk. The staghorn can grow to 1.8 metres (6 ft) in height and spread and the smaller elkorn, 1 metre (3 ft).

GROWING NOTES

For ease of care and handling, and to avoid damaging the underlying surface, mount these ferns on to a backing board. Select hardwood or a purpose-made board from the nursery. Secure the plant with plastic-coated galvanized wire. These slow-growing ferns need little care other than regular moisture and a monthly application of a balanced liquid fertilizer. In cool areas, grow in a greenhouse or conservatory or indoors in a hanging basket, to protect them from the cold. In warm climates they need shelter from hot, drying winds.

Display these magnificent ferns in a prominent spot for bold impact—mount them on an old stump or grow in a hanging basket.

SANSEVIERIA TRIFASCIATA
MOTHER-IN-LAW'S TONGUE, SNAKE PLANT

In warm areas, mother-in-law's tongue does well in a desert or tropical garden, or in pots on a patio. In frost-prone areas, it makes a striking indoor specimen.

Despite its unfortunate name, mother-in-law's tongue is a beautiful plant that looks impressive grown indoors or out. In warm to tropical areas it makes a strong statement mass-planted in a tropical garden or with succulents. Use the straight, boldly variegated succulent leaves as tall exclamation marks, surrounded by a pebble mulch. The lance-shaped leaves, up to 1.2 metres (4 ft) long, can be used to disguise the lower branches of palms or bamboos or to add a spot of foliage colour in a lush green garden. There are many named cultivars with a variety of leaf colours, including 'Laurentii', which has narrow green leaves with bright yellow edges. A dwarf form, 'Compacta', grows to 40 cm (16 inches) high. While its striped leaves are its most striking feature, mother-in-law's tongue produces highly fragrant cream flowers. Indoors, their perfume can be overpowering.

GROWING NOTES

Mother-in-law's tongue is a low-maintenance plant. It tolerates dry conditions and should be allowed to dry out between waterings. As an indoor plant it prefers a brightly lit spot but outdoors it should be sheltered from direct sun.

SARRACENIA SPECIES
PITCHER PLANT

One of nature's most intriguing specimens is the pitcher plant. A native of the peat bogs and wetland areas of North America, the pitcher plant has unique foliage, unusual flowers and a penchant for insects! The way this carnivore captures its prey is truly remarkable—the plant has colourful leafy structures called pitchers; insects are attracted to the nectar at the pitcher's rim. As the insects feed, they slip into the pitcher. Unable to escape, they're gobbled up by enzymes.

The pitcher plant comes in a range of shapes and sizes and stunning colours, including red, green, yellow, bronze and white. It can be grown in pots or containers or in a bog garden. Some species have contrasting veining, adding to their decorative appeal. Along with their fascinating pitchers, these beautiful plants have large-petalled, nodding flowers from spring to early summer. These blooms rise above the pitchers on stems that can stand 60–100 cm (2–3 ft) tall.

Where temperatures fall below –5°C (23°F), grow pitcher plants in a cold or cool greenhouse or on a sunny windowsill.

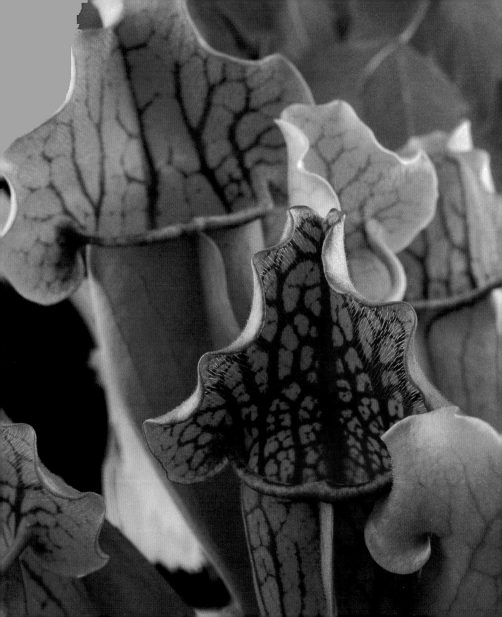

GROWING NOTES

Hardy pitcher plants thrive in climates ranging from cold to subtropical. Some tolerate frost and may even survive under snow while others become dormant in low temperatures. They prefer an open, sunny spot with moist soil. At least six hours of sunlight is ideal, but partial shade is preferred in hot climates.

Plants grow from an underground rhizome. Grow in a mix of peat and river sand in containers. To prevent the mix from drying out, stand pots on a tray of moistened gravel. Also, allow tap water to stand for a day before using on these plants to remove any chlorine. Do not try to trigger the insect traps as this will weaken and possibly kill the plant. Pitchers wither and die in winter, then new ones appear in spring. When removing spent pitchers, take care not to damage any leafy growth or emerging pitchers. Pitcher plants can trap flies, wasps and ants, which are broken down to provide nutrients for the plant.

Curiouser and curiouser... the network of contrasting-coloured veins adds to the appeal of the pitcher plant.

SEDUM MORGANIANUM
BURRO TAIL, DONKEY'S TAIL

For sheer visual splendour, burro tail is a top performer. This striking evergreen perennial features long pendulous stems covered with blue-green interlocking leaves. The plants look their spectacular best when trailed over rocks or spilling out of a hanging basket. When suspended, the stems can hang down to 1–2 metres (3–6 ft) or more. While the plants are grown for their foliage, they do flower in summer, producing pink-red starry flowers at the tips of the stems.

GROWING NOTES

Majestic burro tail blazes its own trail in large hanging baskets, either mass-planted or as individual specimens.

Burro tails may look robust but the tails are brittle and will readily break into segments. Avoid placing hanging baskets where they'll be brushed or knocked, or you'll be constantly picking up broken stems. All is not lost, however, you can use these dislodged segments to grow new plants. Burro tails require full sun and a well-drained soil or potting mix. Plants in containers, such as hanging baskets, prefer a potting mix designed for succulents. Water burro tails only when dry and, in cold zones, reduce watering in winter.

STRELITZIA REGINAE
BIRD OF PARADISE

The brightly coloured bird-like flowers of strelitzia give it the winning edge in the dramatic garden.

Everything about the bird of paradise is dramatic, making it an ideal feature plant in a warm-climate garden. The distinguishing feature of this clump-forming perennial is its vibrant orange and purple flower, which closely resembles an exotic bird. These nectar-rich flowers are also attractive to birds. At 1.2–1.8 metres (4–6 ft) tall and 1 metre (3 ft) wide, the bird of paradise can be used with great effect in the garden—as an exclamation point or lining a wide path or mass-planted for exuberant colour and form. Large clumps can be used to conceal an unsightly outlook or transform a fenceline into a green feature. Give clumps room to spread and accentuate with a mulch of pebbles or low tufty grass.

GROWING NOTES

The bird of paradise likes full sun and well-drained soil in a warm to tropical climate. Plants tolerate some shade, but produce fewer flowers in shady spots. In cool areas, grow bird of paradise as a pot plant in a brightly lit conservatory. Regularly remove spent flowers to make way for new blooms.

YUCCA ELEPHANTIPES
SPINELESS YUCCA, GIANT YUCCA

There are many dramatic yuccas to select as accent or feature plants, but *Yucca elephantipes* has the distinction of being both large and without any sharp spines. The young plants form a dense clump with leaves to the base of the plant. When mature, the plant develops an attractive rough trunk that branches into handsome rosettes of long, shiny green leaves with serrated edges. Plants can grow to 9 metres (30 ft) high but are usually smaller in gardens. The flowers are spires of pretty white bells that bloom from summer to autumn. Use this yucca to mask a fence or present it as a tall feature in an arid or Mediterranean-style garden. Individual plants make exciting potted plants. Highlight the bold, sword-shaped leaves by positioning the pot against a plain wall.

GROWING NOTES

Yuccas need warmth, full sun and well-drained, sandy soils. *Yucca elephantipes* prefers warm to tropical climates. Suckers can be used from the base of the plant to propagate new plants. Plants are drought tolerant when established and are suitable for seaside locations. Remove spent flowering stems.

With age, *Yucca elephantipes* forms a many-branched clump. Remove the lower leaves to reveal the stout trunk.

ZAMIA FURFURACEA
CARDBOARD PALM

The thick, leathery fronds of *Zamia furfuracea* resemble stiff cardboard and provide exciting contrast with other green foliage plants.

Despite its common name of cardboard palm, this plant is not a palm. Its long leaves also resemble fronds, but it's not a fern. The cardboard palm is, in fact, a cycad, one of the plants that were around when dinosaurs roamed the earth. The foliage of this Mexican native emerges from a thick, fleshy trunk to form a handsome clump of tightly overlapping leaves about 1–1.2 metres (3–4 ft) long. Make the most of its shape and texture by growing the cardboard palm where its silver-green leaves (becoming brown underneath) are contrasted with dark-green, lush growth or accentuated against a wall or flat surface. Plants can also be a feature in a large container or in a planter box in a wall garden.

GROWING NOTES

Cycads are long-living, slow-growing plants. Male and female flowers—actually cones—are produced on separate plants. The cardboard palm thrives in warm to tropical climates. In shade its leaflets are flattened but, with increased sun exposure, the individual leaflets can lift up as if folded. Plants need protection from cold and frost, but tolerate seaside conditions.

spires

One sure-fire way to bring height, colour and drama into the garden is to grow plants with tall spires of flowers. Grown as a feature using a couple of specimens, or mass-planted in an array of dazzling colours, spire plants make a showy display in a garden or in containers. Many species have dense foliage, which adds to their appeal. From cottage to formal, spire plants make a big splash.

Spire plants are beautiful to watch during their developing stages. A slender stem emerges from a clump of leaves or sometimes even from a flat rosette. Then the stem gathers momentum, much like Jack's beanstalk, and heads skywards. Later, buds then flowers appear, adding to the spectacle of this gorgeous living sculpture.

Spire plants are particularly effective in cottage or flower gardens. It is here that foxgloves, larkspurs, delphiniums and strident Russell lupins tower above sprawling favourites like geraniums, daisies and lavender. They work well in a Mediterranean climate, too. Handsome silver or grey-leaved verbascums, for example, make a bold statement in a gravel garden or along a gravel path. For an interesting contrast to the tall, vertical shapes, plant some low-growing, rounded succulents or a groundcover like dianthus, or even cover the surrounding area with smooth river pebbles.

With their tall wands of showy flowers, interesting forms and dense foliage, spire plants are also good value in the formal garden. They are at their eye-catching best when clumped dramatically at the top of a set of steps or used as punctuation points alongside a front gate.

Flower spires open from bottom to top for a long-lasting display. Clockwise from top left: Delphinium; foxglove, *Digitalis purpurea*; larkspur, *Consolida ambigua*; and verbascum. Previous page: Russell lupins, *Lupinus* Hybrid Cultivars.

The towering form of the

elegant *Lilium longiflorum*.

Many spire plants can also be happily accommodated in containers. Beautiful specimens like *Lilium* 'Enchantment' and the white Easter lily, *L. longiflorum*, make splendid potted plants. A simple but effective way to dress up the entrance to your home is to have a pair of potted liliums, one on each side of the front door. These exquisite plants bring interest and character to an often stark area.

Although traditional garden wisdom dictates that tall plants should be positioned at the back of a border, or against a wall, it's fun to experiment with them in other situations. Enjoy the sheer height of spires by planting them in the foreground (imagine coming face to face with a row of foxgloves close to a path), or using them to break up a carpet of plants.

Spire plants tend to bloom for weeks or even months. This is because individual flowers open gradually up the spire. And the bonus is, once the main flower spike is finished and removed, a secondary flush may occur.

Many favourite spire flowers are perennials—that is, they grow, flower and die back over a year, usually between spring and autumn. Some, like foxgloves, are biennial—they grow for

Foxgloves bring height and drama in spring.

a year without producing any blooms, then flower the following spring. Although biennials take longer to bloom, their stunning flowers are well worth waiting for.

Along with the traditional spire flowers of European gardens (such as lupins, larkspurs and delphiniums) there are excellent choices for temperate to tropical gardens such as canna, ginger lily (*Hedychium gardnerianum*), true gingers (*Alpinia* species and *Zingiber* species) and the flashy and colourful heliconias. In a warm, shaded garden, display the gorgeous blue ginger, *Dichorisandra thyrsiflora*, with its spires of deep-blue flowers that grow to 2.4 metres (8 ft) high.

GROWING NOTES

Spire plants are not difficult to grow. Those from the traditional cottage garden, such as delphiniums, enjoy a rich, moist soil and, given their height, a spot that is sheltered from strong or drying winds. Plants that favour a Mediterranean climate, such as verbascum, relish full sun and excellent drainage. If you live in an area that's windy or has a heavy rainfall, you'll need to protect the plants during the flowering season. All you need to do is support each plant with a sturdy stake.

Spire plants come in a range of colours and flower shapes.

Clockwise from top left: *Lilium* 'Enchantment'; Jerusalem sage, *Phlomis fruticosa*; *Cardiocrinum giganteum*; and verbascum.

In warm or dry climates, flowering spire plants should be well watered—both in growth and at flowering. If plants are deprived of water, they'll droop and wilt, ruining the overall effect. In sandy, free-draining soils, work in lots of well-rotted organic matter such as compost, leaf mould and aged manure, before planting, to help the soil retain moisture. Water-holding polymers (also called water crystals) can also be added to encourage soils to retain moisture between watering.

Sometimes the dense foliage of a spire plant covers the soil, making it difficult to get water to the root zone. Always check that the water—whether from a hose, watering can or drip irrigation system—falls around the stem of the plant.

Most spire plants relish full sun, but others, like blue ginger, will tolerate shade. In a garden that's shaded in summer and warm and sunny in winter and spring, consider planting foxgloves, which enjoy a woodland garden setting.

Feed fast-growing spire plants regularly as they grow and begin to flower. After flowering, clip off spent stalks to make way for a second flush of flowers. These will not reach the dizzying heights of the first spire, but will continue to bring lively colour and drama to the garden.

Use tall, flowering plants, such as larkspur, to accentuate a garden ornament or curiosity.

ROSETTES

N amed after the perfect form of a rose, the rosette shape appears in the flowers or leaves of a surprisingly wide variety of plants. Whether it's their circular form, the rhythm of overlapping petals or leaves, or the spiralling effect of a whorl, rosettes are visually very stimulating. They're mesmerizingly beautiful, too—because our eyes are drawn to centre of a rosette, they

With hundreds of cultivars, magic neoreglia offers a range of bold designs—stripes, spots, splashes and bands—in rich shades of green, red, burgundy, yellow and pink. Previous pages: Many succulents have tight rosette forms.

make natural focal points in the garden, especially those with large, bold leaves. On a smaller scale, some foliage plants have flower-like radial symmetry; enjoy their beautiful forms by displaying them in pots. Rosette-shaped foliage plants are generally low maintenance as they seldom need pruning. Their neat and tidy appearance will also appeal to those who like order in the garden.

The fronds of *Asplenium australasicum* form a nest, which catches leaves and debris to provide nutrients to the plant. Following pages: The exuberant Japanese sago palm provides spectacular foliage for this water feature.

AEONIUM SPECIES
SAUCER PLANT

Containing every vowel in one tricky word, aeoniums are fortunately much easier to grow than to pronounce. Their common name of saucer or platter plant is much friendlier and describes well the flattish, slightly glossy rosettes of leaves that characterize these succulents. Some species are groundcovers and others form small, branching plants up to 1.5 metres (5 ft) high. Saucer plants also make excellent pot specimens. The wonderful variety of foliage colours includes the purple-black of 'Schwarzkopf', the red, yellow and green of 'Tricolor' and many others in cream, silver and blue-green. A bonus is the showy star-flowers in shades of pink, white red or yellow.

GROWING NOTES

Home for saucer plants is the Canary Islands, northern Africa and the Mediterranean, where they enjoy winter rainfall and dry summers. They tolerate light, but not heavy, frosts and are very reliable in coastal areas and dry areas. Many species can grow in shade, but those with coloured foliage need bright light to maintain their colour. Good drainage is essential.

Like many succulents, saucer plants are undemanding but still provide foliage colour and interest all year round.

AGAVE SPECIES
AGAVE

Soft agaves make showy pot specimens, while their stiff-leaved cousins display their finery as feature plants in the garden.

Agaves provide some of the biggest and boldest rosette shapes in the garden, some sprawling like a giant octopus, others neat and ball-like. They range in height from 30 cm (1ft) to 1.5 metres (5 ft), but the candelabra flower spikes may tower up to 4 metres (13 ft). Their stiff leaves commonly have sharp points that should be removed in pedestrian areas. A popular species, *Agave attenuata*, has no spines and features a perfect, flower-like rosette of soft blue-green foliage. Agaves are ideal for bold accents, or to fill areas that are difficult to access. They suit minimalist gardens and can even be used for formal effects.

GROWING NOTES

Originating from such diverse habitats as deserts and mountains, *Agave* species have varying degrees of frost tolerance. However, they generally withstand wind, heat and drought, and will grow in most soil types as long as they have good drainage. Agaves can take 30 years to flower, after which the flowered rosettes die. These are followed by offsets that mature and flower in subsequent years.

ANANAS SPECIES
PINEAPPLE

One bromeliad that everybody recognizes is the delicious pineapple, *Ananas comosus*. From within the rosette of spiny, grey-green tapering leaves emerges a central flower spike that carries purple-blue flowers and red bracts from late spring to summer. The fruit that forms ripens from dull green to yellow-orange and is especially fragrant when ripe. An ornamental species, *A. bracteatus*, develops intense red colouring on the leaves and bears bright red mini pineapples. Some other forms have striped, variegated leaves and can be grown indoors for their foliage only. Pineapple plants that bear fruit make spectacular pot specimens and a dwarf version can sometimes be purchased at florists.

The distinctive pineapple fruit with its crown of stiff leaves is borne from a rather plain-looking bromeliad. Ornamental variegated foliage forms are also available.

GROWING NOTES
The pineapple plant is strictly for warm climates or a glasshouse, requiring winter temperatures above 10°C (50°F). It needs full sun or very bright light to fruit and an enriched, well-drained soil. Plants can be started from the leafy tops of pineapples. Peel off the lower leaves and allow the tops to dry out before planting between spring and autumn.

ASPLENIUM AUSTRALASICUM
BIRD'S NEST FERN

Bird's nest ferns grow naturally on trees or rocks, making them ideal to grow in difficult, shady areas, such as under trees.

The huge, leathery fronds of *Asplenium australasicum* can grow to 1.5 metres (5 ft) long, forming a nest-like rosette of foliage that adds great drama to a shade garden. The bright green leaves are smooth and glossy, and have a prominent blackish mid-rib. These magnificent ferns look especially attractive against the tree trunks or rocks on which they grow in the wild, or nestled on the forest floor with other, fine-leaved ferns. Their small root system makes them easy to grow anywhere, while the 'nest' catches leaves and other debris to provide nutrients. Grow them near tree ferns (*Dicksonia* spp.), which beautifully echo the circle of foliage, or under trees in groups of three or five. They are also well suited to pot culture.

GROWING NOTES

Bird's nest ferns prefer warm, humid conditions in a frost-free climate. In colder areas, protect them over winter in a conservatory or glasshouse. Full sun will burn the fronds, so choose a position with dappled or filtered light. They need good drainage, but like to be kept reliably moist.

CYCAS REVOLUTA
JAPANESE SAGO PALM

D espite its common name, Japanese sago palm is not a palm at all, but a member of the unique and ancient cycad family—the 'dinosaurs' of the plant world. Cycads have spirally arranged fronds sprouting from thick stems that very slowly develop into trunks. There are separate male and female plants and both bear cones that grow to impressive sizes in the centre of the plant. If pollinated, the seeds are bright orange or red. Japanese sago palm is more tolerant to cold than most cycads and is widely cultivated as a garden or pot specimen. Design-wise, it is amazingly adaptable. From lush foliage and tropical gardens to formal and modern styles, the Japanese sago palm is a top performer.

Japanese sago palms are magnificent sculptural plants; their long arching fronds are on display all year round. They can live for 100 years or more and grow to 3 metres (10 ft) high and 2 metres (6 ft) wide.

GROWING NOTES

Japanese sago palm is easily grown in a wide range of climates from the tropics to cool areas and it tolerates moderate frosts. It takes full sun or partial shade and handles coastal conditions surprisingly well. Use a good-quality potting mix, or a freely drained soil in the garden with added organic matter.

CYCLAMEN
CYCLAMEN

With their clusters of heart-shaped, marbled leaves radiating from a central tuber, cyclamens make a valuable contribution to the foliage garden. But it is their distinctive flowers, with swept-back, slightly twisted petals, that are most admired. The colours can be white, pastels or varying shades of rich pink and crimson. Some have pretty frills, others delicate perfumes. Flowering can occur from autumn to spring, with the bulbs dying back over summer. Use smaller cyclamens, such as *C. hederifolium*, in drifts under deciduous trees or in rock gardens. The florists' cyclamen (*C. persicum*) is used as a flowering pot plant, particularly for indoors. The gorgeous floral display can last for months.

Picture-perfect cyclamens offer a range of glorious colours and interesting foliage. These beauties shine in gardens or in pots.

GROWING NOTES

Cyclamens are best grown in warm or cool temperate climates. Some species are very frost hardy, others are quite tender. Keep potted cyclamens away from draughts and hot, dry air. In gardens, use a light, enriched soil that drains freely. Allow cyclamens to dry out in summer. Tubers can be left undisturbed and plants will usually self-seed freely.

ECHEVERIA SPECIES AND CULTIVARS
HEN AND CHICKS

With its unique form and spectacularly colourful foliage and flowers, echeveria can weave magic in a garden. Leaf hues cover the whole colour spectrum, from silver-blue, grey, pink, mauve and green, to orange, red and brown, with many displaying seasonal colour changes. Leaf surfaces vary too—waxy, velvety or dusted with a white bloom with smooth, pointed or curly edges. Individual rosettes range from 10 cm (4 inches) to 45 cm (18 inches) in diameter, and a few species form branching plants. Echeverias bear spikes of bell-shaped flowers, usually yellow or orange, that are long lasting. They can be used as a interesting groundcover in sheltered spots, but most commonly are grown in pots. They are particularly effective massed in shallow bowls.

GROWING NOTES
Although many echeveria species prefer warm, frost-free conditions, others can stand very cold temperatures as long as the soil is dry. They dislike moisture on their leaves, so thrive under cover on porches and verandahs. Bright light enhances the leaf colours, but many species need a little afternoon shade. Use an open potting mix that drains freely.

Potted, specimen or groundcover, massed echeveria makes a bold statement in any garden.

FESTUCA GLAUCA
BLUE FESCUE

Versatile blue fescue makes a big impact wherever it is used in the garden. It's easy to grow and requires little care.

Forming circular clumps of handsome foliage with an exuberant showy spread, blue fescue is an asset in any garden design. En masse, its ethereal silver-blue foliage looks like a drifting misty haze. Blue fescue works well as an edging for paths or beds—it makes an interesting alternative to mondo grass. Use it as a gorgeous shimmering groundcover, especially where the soil needs binding, or in informal drifts in mixed-foliage beds. Highlight its rosette shape by growing it as a potted specimen, or for filling pockets in a rockery. A mature clump grows to about 30 cm (1 ft) in height and width but there are cultivars that are more compact. Insignificant, slender flower spikes appear in summer.

GROWING NOTES

Blue fescue does best in cool to cold climates and dislikes hot, humid conditions. It withstands severe frosts and tolerates even poor soils as long as it is well drained. Grow it in full sun for the best colour, or with afternoon shade in warmer climates. This hardy plant requires little maintenance apart from the removal of dead leaves.

BRASSICA OLERACEA, ACEPHALA GROUP
KALE

Are these flowers, leaves or vegetables? Ornamental kales are pretty enough to be flowers but are edible relatives of cabbages.

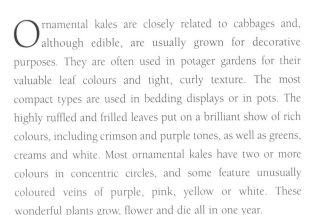

Ornamental kales are closely related to cabbages and, although edible, are usually grown for decorative purposes. They are often used in potager gardens for their valuable leaf colours and tight, curly texture. The most compact types are used in bedding displays or in pots. The highly ruffled and frilled leaves put on a brilliant show of rich colours, including crimson and purple tones, as well as greens, creams and white. Most ornamental kales have two or more colours in concentric circles, and some feature unusually coloured veins of purple, pink, yellow or white. These wonderful plants grow, flower and die all in one year.

GROWING NOTES

Ornamental kales are both cold tolerant and frost hardy. They like a rich, moist soil that is slightly alkaline, and regular applications of liquid fertilizer to encourage rapid growth. Grow them in full sun, keeping watch for snails and caterpillars. Kales can be grown from seed or bought as small potted plants in autumn. These delightful plants are at their spectacular best during autumn and winter.

NEOREGELIA SPECIES AND CULTIVARS
BROMELIADS

Bold and striking neoregelias are high-impact plants. They feature spectacular leaf colours and patterns and, most remarkably, produce a brilliant colour change in the centre of the rosette at flowering time. These colours can be red, pink or purple and persist after the flowers have faded. The flowers are small and insignificant. In contrast, the colourful leaves are stiff and shiny with small spines on the edges. Neoregelias grow on trees or logs, as well as in pots and in the ground. Use them under trees or in locations where they are viewed from above to best appreciate their wonderful form and colour.

GROWING NOTES

Natives of South America, neoregelias need temperatures above 10°C (50°F) to thrive, and dislike any cold rain or frost. Warmth, humidity and bright, but not strong, light will bring out their best performance. Sharp drainage is essential in an open mix to allow the roots to aerate. The central vase should always have water and daily misting helps to increase humidity.

With more than 70 species on offer, neoregelias offer a smorgasbord of sizes, textures and colours. They enjoy humid conditions.

NYMPHAEA SPECIES AND CULTIVARS
WATERLILIES

The hardest thing about growing waterlilies is trying to choose a colour—all are spectacularly beautiful.

Waterlilies have graced our ponds, lakes and water gardens since earliest times. From their simple, circular leaves floating on the water's surface to their elegant blooms, they radiate serenity, harmony and beauty. There are two main groups of waterlilies, tropical and hardy (cold tolerant). These two groups can't be interbred. The tropical varieties carry their flowers on long stems held above the water, and include blue, violet and purple colours that are not found in the hardy varieties. The flowers of the cold-tolerant types float on the water's surface.

There's a wide range of waterlilies on offer, in an even wider range of colours. Dwarf and fragrant cultivars have also been developed. Flowers vary in size from 5 cm (2 inches) in diameter to about 30 cm (12 inches), borne mostly from late spring to late summer. Blooms open during the day and close

Frost-hardy waterlilies grow in most climates and flower throughout summer; the tropical species put on their display from midsummer into autumn.

at night, with the exception of some tropical species that bloom at night. Flowers can be cut to float in a bowl to make an attractive and fragrant display.

Waterlilies grow from a tuber-like rhizome that can be divided and replanted in spring. Most will grow in 30–50 cm (12–20 inches) of water; vigorous varieties will need more water and dwarf types are suited to shallow ponds. Hardy species die back in winter and should be lifted if the pond is likely to freeze to the depth of the rootball.

GROWING NOTES

Waterlilies grow in diverse climates, ranging from the tropics to cold areas, although all tropical varieties are frost tender. Specialist nurseries can recommend the most suitable types for you along with a range of beautiful colours. Fill pots with soil and aged cow manure, rather than potting mix, and cover with a thick layer of pebbles to hold the soil in place. Waterlilies need a sunny position to flower well and like still water.

PHOENIX ROEBELENII
PYGMY DATE PALM

The pygmy or dwarf date palm features a rosette of large and graceful fronds, divided into fine, shiny leaflets. It features a slender trunk and rarely grows more than 3 metres (10 ft) tall. It is particularly useful as an understorey plant with larger palms. Plant it in groups for best effect, or use a tall specimen as an accent. Like most palms, it's easy to grow—its only vice is the sharp spines that replace the lower leaflets at the base of each frond. This makes it safe to brush past, but painful if a hand is thrust into its centre. The pygmy date palm makes an attractive and robust indoor plant or potted specimen on a terrace or balcony.

Delicate yet imposing — the arching, lace-like fronds of the pygmy date palm contrast with the roughly textured trunk.

GROWING NOTES

Originating in Laos, this palm thrives in warm, humid climates. It needs protection from frosts and, although it will survive some dry periods, it prefers ample water in summer. The leaves tend to yellow if grown in full sun, but remain a rich green colour in dappled light or semi-shade.

PRIMULA SPECIES AND HYBRIDS
PRIMULA

Primulas are a diverse group of plants, offering a wide range of lovely colours to brighten up shady and moist areas.

With more than 400 species on offer, there are primulas to suit any season and colour scheme. They feature a tuft or rosette of lush leaves, usually with scalloped or toothed edges, and flower stems carrying whorls or clusters of open-faced flowers. The candelabra primulas (*P. beesiana*, *P. bulleyana* and *P. japonica*) feature showy tiers of flowers that look spectacular growing in large drifts in spring and summer. The blooms die down in winter. Cowslips have yellow perfumed flowers in summer and primroses (derived from *P. vulgaris*) form carpets of colour in spring. Polyanthus (syn. *P.* x *polyantha*) is a cross between a primrose and a cowslip with clusters of colourful flowers held aloft on a short stem. Available in myriad colours, it is popular as a winter-flowering perennial or annual. Use it in small pots, window boxes or as a bedding plant.

GROWING NOTES

Primulas like moist, rich soil and cool or temperate climates. Some species are bog garden plants while others resent winter waterlogging. Primulas prefer a semi-shaded position and slightly alkaline soil. Remove dead heads after flowering.

potted

Where would we be without potted plants? These little marvels are instant gardens that will happily grow in the smallest of spaces and blend in with any landscape. Plants in pots can also tickle our senses with gorgeous colour, interesting forms and amazing textures. They can be practical, too—discover the joys of picking fresh herbs and vegetables from your potted garden.

Potted plants are usually displayed as single specimens, especially when they have dramatic or sculptural form. But, sometimes a single specimen can trigger interest in a particular group of plants, and a small collection grows. For others, success with one plant prompts the acquisition of more, perhaps in different colours. A collection of potted plants is fascinating to observe, too. Watching nature at work and comparing differences and similarities can be all-absorbing.

The collection of plants can be contained within one wide pot—for instance, with succulents or herbs—or may be a grouping of pots, each holding an individual specimen. Where space is limited, a single pot can represent a garden in miniature and be the focal point on an outdoor table.

HERBS AND VEGETABLES

For apartment dwellers, the kitchen garden is a potted affair. And the benefit of having pots in a garden setting is that it gives plants mobility; they can be moved around throughout the year for shelter or sun. A surprising variety of herbs and vegetables grow happily in pots, looking attractive as well as being productive. Herbs should be grouped according to their cultural requirements. For instance, the Mediterranean herbs,

A colony of potted plants instantly adds style and grace to any landscape. Clockwise from top left: herbs and lavender; rosettes of echeverias complement a round pot; red *Dianthus barbatus* and flowering echeveria make a pretty combination; and ivy-and-candle decoration.

Quick-growing and hardy, succulents perform well in most climates. A small collection puts on a showy display in pots or rockeries—and looks spectacular in a clam shell.

such as rosemary, thyme, oregano and sage, need full sun and to be kept fairly dry. Other lush green, leafy herbs, like basil, parsley, chives and rocket, need a richer potting mix as well as ample water and fertilizer to give their best. Most leafy salad greens grow to perfection in pots, especially on a cut-and-come-again basis, and look fabulous as a collection in a wide bowl or trough.

There are lots of delicious vegetables that will happily grow in pots, including cherry tomatoes, chillies, capsicums, dwarf French beans, lettuces, bunching shallots (spring onions), radishes, eggplants and dwarf carrots.

This easy-care potted garden, containing a variety of succulents, offers colour, form and texture in one neat little package.

SUCCULENTS AND CACTI

An easy way to add interesting colour, texture and form to the garden is to plant a collection of different varieties of cacti and succulents. Cacti work very well set up as a miniature garden with branching tree-like forms, balls and other shapes. Succulents offer the greatest variety of leaf colours, shapes and textures. Sempervivums, aeoniums and echeverias provide endless scope for potted collections that look good all year round. These mini gardens make a wonderful display for an outdoor table setting. Shallow bowls, especially in terracotta, suit these plants perfectly. When the plants are in place, spread a layer of decorative pebbles or gravel on top of the soil to reduce humidity. The stones also complete the picture.

GRASSES

Grasses are increasingly popular, both for their wonderful style and ease of cultivation. Because of their clumping and spreading habit, they are best grown in individual pots and displayed as a collection. For a striking display, choose contrasting foliage colours and textures, then plant in matching pots. Some favourites are black mondo grass (*Ophiopogon planiscapus* 'Nigrescens'), blue fescue (*Festuca glauca*), Japanese blood grass (*Imperata cylindrica* 'Rubra'), variegated ribbon grass (*Phalaris arundinacea* var. *picta*), dwarf New Zealand flax (*Phormium*) and lily turf (*Liriope*).

The pots can be grouped informally, with taller grasses at the back and the smaller varieties at the front, or arranged in a row to make a statement. Matching pots can also look impressive marching up and down a set of steps.

CHOOSING CONTAINERS

The type of container in which you grow your plants is limited only by your imagination. The one requirement is that you have sufficient drainage holes.

Pots are available in a wide range of materials, including plastics, terracotta, glazed ceramic, stone, imitation stone and marble. There are also colours and styles to suit any garden. Less conventional, but probably more exciting, are recycled objects such as old wheelbarrows, boots, clam shells, olive oil tins, wine barrels, chimney pots—even the laundry sink.

Grasses are easy to grow in pots, as long as they have good drainage. Topping the pots with pebbles or gravel not only looks attractive but is also quite practical. It helps to keep the roots cool and reduces any humidity around the foliage.

Clockwise from top left: flax lily; *Carex oshimensis*; mixed grasses; and *Phalaris arundinacea* var. *picta*.

Plants with small root systems, such as cacti and succulents, can be grown in wide, shallow pots. This way you can grow a collection of plants in one container. Shallow pots will dry out quickly, but the dry conditions suit cacti and succulents. Vegetables, such as carrots and beans, need much deeper pots to provide the necessary root space and to ensure there is a plentiful food and water supply to fuel the plants' growth.

GROWING NOTES

Always use a good-quality potting mix, or a specialist mix for plants such as cacti and succulents. Pay close attention to watering, as plants in pots dry out much faster than those in a garden and, the smaller the pot, the faster the plant dries out. As terracotta is more porous than other materials it will dry out more quickly. Water-storing crystals and soil-wetting agents can help to keep soil in pots evenly moistened. These products are ideal for those plants that do not like to dry out.

It's important to use either soluble or controlled-release fertilizers for potted plants, as those that are suitable for gardens can be too potent for pots. The application depends on the plants you are growing. Soluble fertilizers can be applied to vegetables every two weeks to promote rapid growth, but cacti may only need to be fed once or twice a year.

When choosing your pots or containers, think about matching the style of container to the plants. Here, a miniature waterlily grows well in a deep bowl.

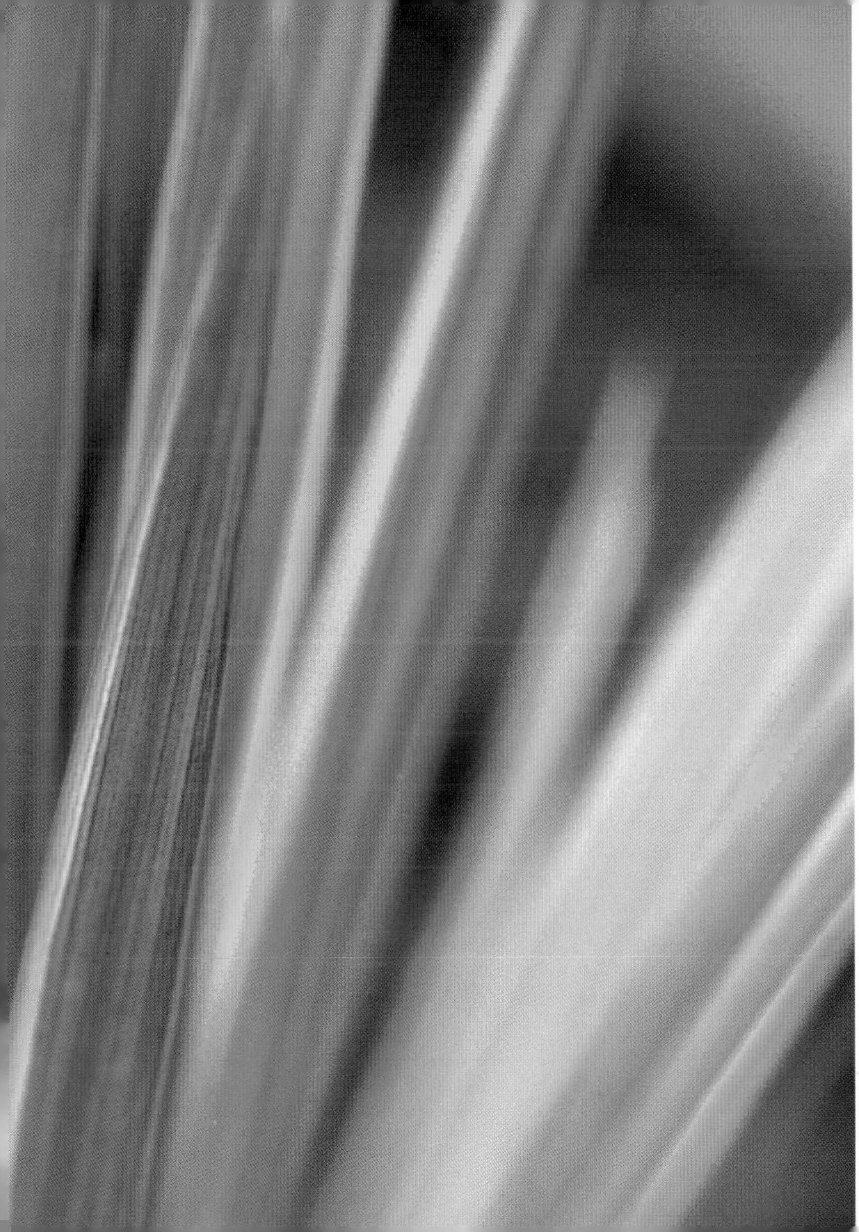

SPIKY

F irst reactions might be that spiky plants are not something you would want in the garden, but spiky doesn't have to mean thorny or prickly. To dismiss spiky plants is to miss out on a wealth of marvellous texture, shape and form in the garden. The interesting shapes of some of the plants we have selected in this chapter come into their own when viewed against a background

Tufts of spiky foliage, used in a mass planting, are an excellent textural contrast in the garden. Torch lilies fit the bill and also offer fabulous flower spikes in hot colours. Previous pages: The spectacular foliage of cordyline.

of small or regular foliage. They add the important punctuation points that break up what can be just a bland expanse of garden or wall. Of course, some plants have real spines or thorns, which are usually a defence against being eaten. But, these can work for you in the garden to keep out unwanted animals or to form a security barrier.

Use striking spiky plants, such as sea holly (left) or agave (right), as features alongside a pathway.
Following pages: The pretty white, mauve and yellow flowers of wild iris appear to float on a sea of foliage.

AECHMEA SPECIES AND CULTIVARS
AECHMEA

From the plant family that brought us the pineapple, aechmea is one of the easiest and most rewarding bromeliads to grow. With more than 170 species and many more cultivars, there is a wonderful choice of leaf colour and patterns—bands, streaks, blotches and spots in rich shades of green, red, burgundy, silver, yellow and gold. The long-lasting flowers are no less exotic with their range of brilliant colours and dramatic shapes. The vase-like shape formed by their stiff rosette of leaves acts as a water reservoir, and many species have little spines along the leaf margins. Colourful berry fruits follow the flowers and persist for a long period.

Versatile and undemanding, aechmea can be mass-planted under trees, mounted on a log or used as a stunning feature in a pot.

GROWING NOTES

Most aechmeas are either rock dwellers or epiphytes, with a penchant for the forks of trees. They can be mounted on small logs, or grown in a coarse open mix in pots or even in the ground where excellent soil drainage is essential. They prefer a warm and humid climate, but will tolerate cold temperatures as long as there is no frost. Choose a sheltered position with dappled light. In very cold climates, grow them indoors.

ALOE SPECIES AND CULTIVARS
ALOES

M ost people know of *Aloe vera*, the wonderful healing plant, used extensively in medicines and cosmetics. The clear sap from its fleshy, slightly spiny leaves can be smeared directly onto burnt skin to give instant relief. But, there are more than 300 other species, some as large as trees, and all with succulent, stalkless leaves. The tree-like species add large, sculptural forms to the garden, while many smaller types make interesting clumps. Mature aloe plants produce stems of red, orange or yellow flowers, usually in winter to spring, that attract honey-eating birds. *Aloe saponaria* has sap that foams in water and is used as a substitute for soap.

GROWING NOTES

There are aloes that come from both cool temperate regions and tropical deserts, but only a few species tolerate frosts and most prefer a warm, dry climate. Larger species do best in full sun, but others can take semi-shade. All aloes must have very good drainage. They can survive in poor soils but need a coarse, open potting mix if grown in containers.

Above: Many aloes feature attractive stems of nectar-rich flowers, usually in orange, yellow or red. Opposite: *Aloe vera* may look a little scary, but the succulent leaves are full of soothing sap than can ease burns and abrasions.

ANIGOZANTHOS SPECIES AND CULTIVARS
KANGAROO PAW

The tubular flowers of kangaroo paw attract nectar-eating birds. Mass-planting gives the greatest impact, with bold sweeps of colour from spring.

This distinctively Australian flower not only resembles the shape of a kangaroo's paw, it's also delightfully furry in texture. The bold clumps of shiny, sword-shaped leaves make a dramatic textural contribution to the garden, but the show is really on when the flower spikes reach skywards in shades of ochre, red, orange, pink and green. Recent breeding has produced a range of hybrids—small, 30–60 cm (1–2 ft), medium, 60–120 cm (2–4 ft) and tall 1–2 metres (3–6 ft). Flowering is mainly from late spring to summer, although some dwarf cultivars will flower most of the year in temperate climates. These are suitable for growing in pots.

GROWING NOTES

Kangaroo paw is suited to temperate and subtropical climates, tolerating light frosts and coastal exposure. It is adaptable to most soil types, as long as it drains freely. Full sun is the other basic requirement. It performs best if given regular water when growing actively from autumn through winter, and in spring when the buds are forming. Remove spent flower stems at ground level to encourage new growth.

BILLBERGIA SPECIES AND CULTIVARS
VASE PLANT

The gracefully arching flower spikes of the vase plant are a dominant feature of these widely grown bromeliads. They have large and colourful bracts, usually pink or red, which enclose small petals of blue, purple or green. The long, strap-like leaves are arranged around a central cup that acts as a water reservoir. Leaf colours include green, maroon, pink, silver and cream, often mottled, spotted or banded, and many have small spines along the leaf margins. Use them as a massed groundcover under trees, or in tree branches where they can be displayed to best advantage.

Form, foliage and showy flowers add to the appeal of easily grown billbergia.

GROWING NOTES
In tropical and subtropical climates, billbergia grows very well, but in cooler areas it should be grown in glasshouses or indoors. It needs temperatures above 5°C (41°F) and a position with high light levels but sheltered from hot sun. Growing naturally in trees, it needs a fast-draining soil mix but otherwise is not fussy about conditions. Mist potted and indoor specimens regularly to increase humidity.

CORDYLINE AUSTRALIS
NEW ZEALAND CABBAGE TREE

The versatile New Zealand cabbage tree makes a striking feature plant in gardens, growing to 6 metres (20 ft) high. However, it is more often seen as a juvenile where it is used as an indoor or potted plant. This frost-hardy beauty features an upright plume of stiff, sword-shaped leaves that arch gently as they age. When planted in the ground, it develops a stout trunk and begins to branch after flowering. The species has mid-green leaves but several cultivars feature cream-and-pink striped or purple foliage. Mature plants produce a large panicle of sweetly scented, small, white flowers in summer. These are followed by white to mauve berries.

GROWING NOTES

Moderately frost hardy, this cabbage tree suits warm temperate and subtropical regions. It will tolerate salt spray, full sun and strong winds, but makes a better specimen with some shelter. With good drainage it is easy to grow and suffers few pest or disease problems. Pot plants need regular summer water and will grow in part shade or full sun.

Cordyline australis is a structural specimen tree when mature, but is also used as a no-fuss pot plant for terraces and indoors.

CROCUS SPECIES AND HYBRIDS
CROCUS

Crocus is one of the most delicately beautiful bulbs, small in size but big on charm. Some of the 80 or so species are harbingers of spring, pushing their blooms up through snow, while others flower in autumn. The best known is *Crocus sativus*, whose orange stigmas are the source of the costly spice saffron. Its flowers are mauve, but crocus can be white, pink, blue or yellow, and many have fine stripes or feathering on the petals. The foliage is grass-like and sparse. Mass-plant crocus under deciduous trees and in lawns or place clusters in rockeries and pots. Sadly, the blooms are not long lasting in a vase.

The small, goblet-shaped blooms of crocus have a delightful elfin quality and look their best when naturalized in the garden.

GROWING NOTES
Despite its fragile appearance, crocus thrives in cool to cold areas and may fail to flower if the climate is too warm. *Crocus salzmannii* can be grown in warmer areas. Choose an open, sunny position with very well drained soil, enriched with organic matter. Bulbs can be lifted and divided every three to four years or when the area becomes overcrowded. They can be grown in pots in warm areas, in a cool spot.

CYNARA CARDUNCULUS
CARDOON

Related to both the humble thistle and the edible globe artichoke, the cardoon is a magnificent accent plant in every respect. Its sumptuous silver-grey leaves are deeply divided with well-defined veins and spiny edges. Forming a large clump to around 2 metres (6 ft) wide and high, cardoons need plenty of space to make their impact. The distinctive mauve flowers crown the plant in summer on towering stems up to 3 metres (9 ft) tall, and can be dried for decoration indoors. The leaf stalks are edible. Cardoon is a herbaceous perennial, dying back in winter. Use it against a background of darker foliaged shrubs to set off its sculptural qualities.

GROWING NOTES
The ideal climate for growing cardoon is hot, dry summers and cold, wet winters. In warm areas, the plants won't fully die down in winter and can be pruned away instead. Grow them in full sun, in well-drained soil, heavily enriched with compost and manure. Separate and replant the offsets that form around the crown in early spring.

Big, bold and beautiful cardoon has loads of character—silvery foliage, distinctive flowers and a unique textural appeal.

CYPERUS SPECIES
PAPYRUS, UMBRELLA SEDGE

Cyperus forms stately clumps that provide strong, vertical accents in shallow ponds. The long-lasting, decorative flowers occur in summer.

W ater-loving *Cyperus* species, at home in a shallow pond or in moist ground, make striking accent plants. Their slender stems, topped with umbrella-like heads of narrow leaves, move gracefully in a gentle breeze and create dynamic reflections in the water. *Cyperus papyrus* was used by the ancient Egyptians to make a form of paper. This species produces stems up to 3 metres (9 ft) high with fine, starburst heads, and forms dense clumps. *C. involucratus*, the umbrella sedge, grows to about 1 metre (3 ft) high, with flat heads of narrow leaves, and yellowish spikelets of flowers in the centre.

GROWING NOTES

Cyperus loves warm and tropical climates, although papyrus will tolerate temperatures almost to freezing and umbrella sedge grows in cool climates if they are frost free. Both grow in almost any soil, in full sun or partial shade, as long as it is constantly moist. They can be over-vigorous in rich soils, due to their spreading habit, but the underground runners are easily severed or can be confined in a pot.

DIERAMA PULCHERRIMUM
ANGEL'S FISHING ROD

Sometimes a plant's common name is absolutely perfect, and so it is with the delicate, arching stems of *Dierama pulcherrimum*. The silvery pink, bell-shaped flowers dance daintily in the gentlest breeze. Also available are the deep pink and white forms. Clumps of evergreen, sword-shaped leaves grow to around 50 cm (20 inches), but the slender flower stems may be more than twice as high. Use them in informal groups, or dotted along the edge of a pond where reflections can double their magic. Native to South Africa, angel's fishing rod grows from a corm and flowers in late spring to summer.

No guessing where the common name came from. *Dierama* produces fine wiry flower stems that bend like fishing rods under the weight of its flower clusters.

GROWING NOTES
Marginally frost hardy, angel's fishing rod grows well in a warm temperate climate but succeeds in cooler areas when given a sheltered position. Flowering is best in full sun. It needs a rich, well-drained soil with regular watering during spring and summer. Large clumps can be divided in autumn or winter, but this plant resents any disturbance and it can take a year or more before it begins to flower again.

DIETES SPECIES
WILD IRIS
FORTNIGHT LILY

Combining a tough-as-nails attitude and delicate-looking flowers, *Dietes* is a valuable plant for difficult spots. It tolerates pollution and neglect and, once established, will self seed freely. The slender, sword-shaped leaves form erect clumps about 1 metre (3 ft) tall, serving as a perfect foil for the iris-like blooms. *D. bicolor* has pale yellow petals, the three largest of which have a central brown spot. *D. grandiflora* bears profuse white-and-mauve flowers with yellow spots. Flowering is almost constant from spring through summer, although individual blooms last only a day or two. Use them as accent plants, under trees, or to line a driveway.

Bold form and gorgeous flowers make the wild iris appealing, but its real strength is its toughness. *Dietes grandiflora* (top and opposite); *Dietes bicolor* (above).

GROWING NOTES

Native to South Africa, wild iris is marginally frost hardy, but is not fussy about soil type. While preferring some moisture, it can tolerate long, dry periods as well as wind and coastal exposure. All species thrive in full sun or partial shade, but flowering is more prolific in a sunny position. Large clumps can be dug and divided, ideally in spring.

ERYNGIUM SPECIES
SEA HOLLY

Sea holly's dominant feature is its metallic-like sheen. Colours vary from steely blue and greenish white to a deep mauve.

Sea holly adds marvellous texture and colour to a mixed border. Both leaves and flowers of this striking perennial are spiky and have unusual shapes and colouring. The flowers feature a small, dense cone surrounded by a prominent ruff of spiny bracts. The whole plant has an enchanting silvery blue sheen. Some forms are bluer than others and combine particularly well with yellow and orange flowers planted nearby. Particularly striking is the purplish blue *Eryngium alpinum* with its soft bracts. Most species grow to around 1 metre (3 ft) high. Summer-flowering eryngiums make stunning plants for naturalizing. They also look attractive as a border or they can be cut and dried for indoor arrangements.

GROWING NOTES

Sea holly comes from South America and Europe and is mostly frost hardy, making it suitable for subtropical to temperate climates. It develops its best colour in full sun and dislikes wet soils, particularly in winter. Sandy soils provide the necessary free drainage. Cut it back late in the season if it is looking untidy.

EUPHORBIA MILII
CROWN OF THORNS

Few shrubs are as fiercely thorny as the aptly named crown of thorns. In the same genus as the similarly bright red poinsettia, the crown of thorns features semi-succulent stems that are covered in long, sharp spines. The small leaves are evergreen in warmer climates but may be sparse or even deciduous in colder areas. The true flowers are tiny and yellowish, but are surrounded by red bracts that are long lasting. There is also a white-flowered form. Flowering peaks in spring and summer, but often continues throughout the year. With a height of 30–40 cm (12–16 inches) and a spreading habit, crown of thorns makes a colourful hedge and an excellent barrier to deter unwanted visitors.

GROWING NOTES
A native of Madagascar, crown of thorns needs a warm to hot climate and performs well in arid areas. Give it full sun and any free-draining soil. The succulent stems make it tolerant to drought and heat once the plant is established.

Beautiful on top, ferocious below, the bright red blooms of crown of thorns provide a long-lasting display that sits above impenetrable spines.

ILEX SPECIES AND CULTIVARS
HOLLY

The common holly (above) has pretty white flowers followed by red berries in autumn and winter. Many cultivars have variegated leaves that feature gold, cream or silver highlights.

Evergreen holly is such an adaptable, useful and dependable plant that, even without its familiar show of red berries for Christmas in the Northern Hemisphere, we would welcome it into our gardens. Left to its own devices, common or English holly, *Ilex aquifolium*, forms a shapely tree to about 10 metres (30 ft) in height. More commonly, it makes a fine hedge that not only provides dense screening, but also keeps out unwelcome visitors. The glossy leaves are characteristically spiny in most varieties and can be deep green, or variegated in gold or cream. The foliage is popular with florists, as it provides a perfect foil to brightly coloured flowers and is also long lasting. Holly is a good container plant and specimen shrub, and is suited to topiary work.

Male and female flowers are produced on separate plants. Both are needed for berry production, although there are some self-fertile cultivars; and only the females bear berries. Flowers

in summer are followed by a brilliant display of berries, ripening from autumn into winter, in red, orange or yellow.

English holly, *Ilex aquifolium*, has spawned dozens of cultivars of varying height, shape, leaf and berry colours. It even has some almost thornless forms. For smaller gardens Chinese holly, *I. cornuta*, is popular, being more compact but with larger leaves. This self-fertile species is a better choice for warmer areas; it also produces large berries in summer. Japanese holly, *I. crenata*, has much smaller leaves and black berries. Both species have many cultivars.

Holly has been grown for centuries and has been used in hedging since ancient times. It is also widely used in topiary. This popular plant was sacred to pre-Christian deities well before it became associated with Christmas festivities.

GROWING NOTES

Holly is at its best in cool to cold climates, but will also tolerate warmer zones. Once established, most species are tough enough to cope with snow, winds, pollution and drought, but holly needs regular deep watering in dry weather. Holly doesn't like to be transplanted. Give it a rich, well-drained loam and a position in full sun to promote berry production.

IRIS, BEARDED HYBRIDS
IRIS

Painters, such as French impressionist Claude Monet, have immortalized the iris—they wanted to capture the elegance, colours, strength and beauty of the flowers. Bearded irises are the most widely grown group of iris species, hybrids and cultivars. They have evergreen, silvery, sword-shaped leaves that arise from fat rhizomes. In late spring and summer, sturdy flower stems bear a series of silky-petalled blooms in a myriad of colours. The iris features three outer petals or falls that cascade downwards and three inner petals, or standards, that curve inwards and upwards. The beard refers to a tuft of fine hairs on the falls. Standards and falls can display different colours and patterns in the hundreds of named cultivars, each more beautiful than the last.

The bearded iris is the perfect plant package—it has elegant blooms in a full palette of gorgeous colours, delightful fragrance and handsome, silvery green foliage.

GROWING NOTES
Bearded irises are suited to temperate climates and demand dry feet. They are easy to grow as long as they have full sun and an alkaline, free-draining soil. Plant with the rhizome showing just above soil level and divide clumps every three to four years, discarding the old, central rhizomes.

KNIPHOFIA SPECIES AND CULTIVARS
TORCH LILY, RED-HOT POKER

Big, bold and beautiful, torch lilies are hard to miss in any garden. With their majestic spires of densely packed, tubular flowers, soaring to heights of up to 2 metres (6 ft), they create enormous impact with very little effort. Their fiery colours include red, orange and yellow, and, more recently, pink and white. Most cultivars flower in the warm months, peaking in midsummer, but others bloom in winter and spring. The nectar-rich blooms are attractive to birds and also make long-lasting cut flowers. Torch lilies form large tufts of long grass-like leaves that remain evergreen in all but cool areas. Use torch lilies to add sizzle to a mixed border, as a bold feature or in a mass planting.

The show-stopping spires of torch lilies add glowing warmth and strong vertical elements to the garden. The clumping, grassy foliage offers rich texture.

GROWING NOTES

Most warm and cool climates are suitable for growing torch lilies but some cultivars are more frost hardy than others. They can tolerate poor soils but definitely not wet soils, especially in winter. Plant them in an open position that's in full sun. They can cope with wind, drought and coastal exposure. The clumps of torch lilies are best left undisturbed for many years.

LOMANDRA LONGIFOLIA
MAT RUSH

Decorative flower spikes are a feature of the clump-forming mat rush, which thrives on neglect.

Native to Australia, mat rush is the epitome of a tough, easy-care plant. Its large, tussocky clumps can be up to a metre (3 ft) high and wide and are ideal for filling large, difficult areas that get very little maintenance. This hardy species makes an excellent accent plant and looks particularly effective when positioned among large rocks. The long, slender leaves are very tough, and may be shiny dark green or slightly bluish. From early spring to summer, the flower spikes bear tiny, densely packed cream flowers, with small spines at the base of each cluster. Mat rush has a sweet, honey fragrance.

GROWING NOTES

The adaptable mat rush is suitable for warm to subtropical climates and will also tolerate cooler conditions with light frosts. It grows in almost any type of soil, from sand to rich loam, with reasonable drainage. The mat rush enjoys full sun and coastal exposure, but the leaves will be a deeper green if grown in semi-shade. Although it is very drought tolerant, once established, it makes a better specimen if it is watered occasionally during dry spells. It grows easily from seed.

MAHONIA SPECIES
MAHONIA

Mahonias offer something of interest all year round, with beautiful foliage, yellow, often fragrant, flowers and decorative and long-lasting fruit.

With spiny leaflets reminiscent of holly, mahonias contribute valuable texture to a planting scheme. They are valued equally for their attractive flowers and fruits, and their undemanding ways. Mostly evergreen shrubs to around 2 metres (6 ft), they have multi-stemmed growth, bearing large, handsome leaves that often develop purple or burgundy hues in winter. Sprays of bright yellow flowers, often fragrant, are produced in winter or spring, depending on the species, and are followed by highly decorative, blue-black or red berries. These often have a whitish bloom and resemble small grapes, hence the common name for *M. aquifolium* of grape holly. Use mahonias to make an interesting textural feature, or as a screening hedge or background shrub. Mahonias are elegant displayed against a masonry wall such as in a courtyard.

GROWING NOTES

Mahonias prefer cool, moist climates and tolerate frosts, but are not recommended for very warm areas. Grow them in dappled light, or with protection from afternoon sun or in a sunny spot in cooler areas. They like well-drained soil, rich in organic matter, and a mulch over the roots in summer. Keep them well watered during summer.

MELIANTHUS MAJOR
HONEY BUSH

The beauty of *Melianthus* is in its luscious foliage. Its huge leaves, pinnately divided into gently drooping leaflets, are edged with a neat zigzag pattern. The colours, too, are appealing, in shades of silvery blue and grey-green with purplish hues on the edges of the new growth. Honey bush is grown mainly as a background foliage plant because it has a spreading habit that can be untidy. In warm climates it is evergreen, but in cooler areas it is grown as a herbaceous perennial, the thick, hollow stems shooting rapidly in spring. Its common name comes from the nectar-rich flowers borne from spring to midsummer. The majestic flower spikes are held aloft the plant, thickly clustered with the tubular, burgundy-red blooms that are attractive to birds.

GROWING NOTES
As a native of South Africa, honey bush is best suited to warmer, frost-free climates. In cooler climates, the crown and roots must be protected over winter. A rich, moist soil provides lush growth and full sun produces strong foliage colour.

Evergreen honey bush grows to more than 2 metres (6 ft) tall and forms thick clumps of decorative foliage. The nectar-filled flower spikes add to the splendour.

PACHYPODIUM LAMEREI
MADAGASCAR PALM

It may look like a 'freaked-out' palm, but it is no relation. However, should you be lucky enough to see, and smell, the Madagascar palm in flower, its similarity to the frangipani is unmistakable. The flowers have a similar shape and colour—white with a yellow throat—and a delightful fragrance. The single trunk is sometimes bottle-shaped and is densely covered in sharp spines. With age, it develops a few thick branches, each topped with a whorl of long, leathery leaves. In the wild, it may reach up to 6 metres (18 ft) high, but is more commonly grown as a pot plant, either indoors or out. It makes a dramatic feature plant for gardens that use little water.

Not for tree-huggers, this curious plant nevertheless has excellent form, texture and sculptural value, as well as delightful flowers.

GROWING NOTES

Ideally, the Madagascar palm needs temperatures above 10°C (50°F) in a hot, dry climate. It may lose its leaves in the dry season, and pot plants should barely be watered during winter. Give them full sun outdoors and a brightly lit indoors position. Drainage must always be exceptional to avoid root rot.

TILLANDSIA SPECIES
AIR PLANT

Tillandsia is the largest genus in the Bromeliad family and includes some weird and fabulous plants. Most have very few roots and grow on trees in the wild, absorbing water and nutrients through their leaves. One interesting species is *T. usneoides,* Spanish moss, which hangs in long, silver curtains from branches without the need for soil or a root system. Many species have narrow, tufting foliage, often with fuzzy, silver scales that provide protection from adverse conditions such as frost and dry heat. The blooms can be exotic, like those of *T. lindenii,* with their pink paddles edged with violet-blue flowers. Grow them on trees or fixed to driftwood, rocks or logs.

GROWING NOTES

Tillandsia is mostly from southern and central America, with a wide variety of habitats covering arid, humid, warm and frosty areas. The stiff, silver-leaved species need full sun and the softer, green or reddish foliage types thrive in filtered light. Use a coarse orchid mix if growing in pots and mist the foliage regularly. Water moderately in summer.

The magic air plant offers colour and spectacular form: *T. lindenii* (top); *T. fasciculata* (above); *T. usneoides* and *T. argentea* (opposite).

YUCCA SPECIES
YUCCA

Yuccas have few equals for sheer boldness and an ability to thrive on neglect. They make ideal architectural specimens in a border or courtyard. Yuccas have sword-like leaves arranged in a rosette and some, with age, will develop a central stem or even branches. Spectacular flower spikes erupt high above the foliage in summer or autumn, packed with white or cream bell-shaped flowers. Leaves can be silvery, blue-green, purple-tinged or striped in gold or silver. They make excellent container specimens requiring little care. The flowers of *Y. elephantipes* are even edible.

Yuccas are excellent structural plants, particularly in dry areas. Many small varieties are suited to tub culture.

GROWING NOTES
Yuccas prefer dry climates and while many species can tolerate hard frosts, others need a gentler climate. They are not fussy about soil type as long as it is freely drained. An open position will give them the sun they need as well as room to showcase their striking forms. Keep them fairly dry in winter.

cacti

All too readily the humble cactus is simply dismissed as an unattractive prickly plant that grows in deserts. But nothing could be further from the truth! As you'll discover, cacti have a lot to offer the garden landscape no matter what the climate. They come in a rich variety of sizes, shapes, colours and textures, some produce spectacular flowers and others look hot in the pot. Enjoy.

Cacti are part of the larger group of succulents, distinguished by particular features. These include ribbed surfaces that allow the plant to shrink as it loses water, waxy coatings to reduce water evaporation and, of course, most of them have spines. The spines are actually modified leaves that protect the plant from grazing animals and provide some shade for the fleshy parts of the plant.

Cacti are also distinguished by their unique growing points, known as areoles. These are small woolly cushions from which the groups of spines and flowers emerge. Many species have tubercles, which are warty protrusions.

Their special modifications are a result of the very harsh conditions that these plants endure. On the desert plains, scorching daytime temperatures are followed by freezing nights, and rainfall can be less than 25 mm (1 inch) per year. The cacti that grow in higher elevations survive snow and icy winds, often growing in tiny pockets of soil or even rock crevices. Some species are rainforest plants, including the orchid cactus (*Epiphyllum*) and crab cactus (*Schlumbergera*). They have large, green, flattened stems that are more suited to a humid, milder environment and do not have spines.

Previous page: A cactus garden can dress up a dry-climate garden.
Opposite: Cacti have amazing coping mechanisms, such as their network of spines, which grow from areoles. The spines deter animals from feeding on the water-filled plants and also provide shade for the cacti.

Cacti are suited to growing in pots because it keeps them dry and freely drained. And their fascinating shapes and flowers are often best appreciated when in pots.

The contrast between the austerity of a cactus plant and the flamboyant brilliance of its flowers is a source of wonder. The petals have a silky texture and are yellow, pink or red.

There are three main types of cacti: round or barrel (such as *Echinocactus* and *Mammillaria* species); tall and columnar (such as *Epostoa* and *Cleistocactus* species); and jointed (*Opuntia*, including prickly pear and *Schlumbergera*, the crab cactus).

The surprising bonus with cacti is their fabulous flowers. In sharp contrast to the austerity of the plants, the blooms are vibrant, large and showy, and usually in brilliant colours. They are all the more precious for being so brief, as most have only a day or two of glory. Some are even nocturnal, opening in the depths of night with seductive perfumes to be pollinated by moths or bats, and fading by dawn. Cactus fruits are often brightly coloured and long-lasting.

Cacti make attractive container plants, too, especially planted in terracotta or glazed ceramic pots. Some larger species will look better as single specimens, while a collection of smaller types in a shallow bowl makes a delightful miniature garden. Repetition looks stylish, so consider a group of similar types in pots or perhaps a row of three (of the same type) along the wall of a balcony or on a kitchen windowsill. One advantage of growing your collection in pots is that you can bring them into prime viewing position when the plants are in flower.

A dedicated cactus garden, featuring plants of different shapes and sizes, provides a dramatic landscape in dry, hot environments. The cactus garden can also work well in exposed, difficult spots where other plants would struggle. Make the most of the fascinating sculptural shapes and use cacti as focal points in Mediterranean- or Mexican-themed gardens. And, for extra colour, texture and interest, combine cacti with other succulents. For example, tall columnar cacti such as *Cereus* species contrast well with softer, more pendulous plants like *Echeveria pulvinata*. The soft crab and orchid cacti blend readily with most garden styles and are particularly beautiful when cascading over a hanging basket.

A first cactus purchase is usually the first of many, as their spectacular forms, jewel-like flowers and ease of growing quickly become addictive.

GROWING NOTES

The drier the climate, the better for growing cacti. Low humidity and low rainfall, especially in winter, are ideal. Choose a position with as much sun as possible and good air movement. If you can achieve this under the eaves of a house, the plants will be protected from rain, which is beneficial.

The three rules for successful cactus growing are drainage, drainage and drainage. Perfectly adapted to survive the

The fascination of cacti lies in the diversity of shapes, which range from a minute ball, whose perfection is only revealed in close-up, to towering columns that dominate the landscape.

harshest of environments, they are most often killed by kindness. In pots, use a special cactus mix that has very sharp drainage. Choose a pot that is not much larger than the rootball and check there are sufficient drainage holes. Spread a layer of pebbles or gravel around the top of the pot. This not only looks attractive, but it also reduces humidity around the plants. Lift the pot above the ground with 'pot feet' or pieces of tile to allow air to circulate freely and ensure drainage is not impeded. In the garden, plant cacti in raised beds, in a mix that is three parts sand or crushed stone to one part organic soil, or plant them on a slightly raised mound.

Cacti should only be watered when the soil is quite dry. Overwatering quickly causes rotting and inevitable death. Use a soil-moisture meter if you are unsure, or check the weight of the pot—it will be much lighter when the soil has dried out. Water in the morning rather than evening, to allow excess water to evaporate, and apply enough water to wet all the soil. Cacti do not need much fertilizer. Apply a low-nitrogen, slow-release fertilizer in spring, using perhaps slightly less than the recommended amount. Plants can be brought indoors for short periods, but need a very brightly lit situation to survive indoors if they are there for the long term.

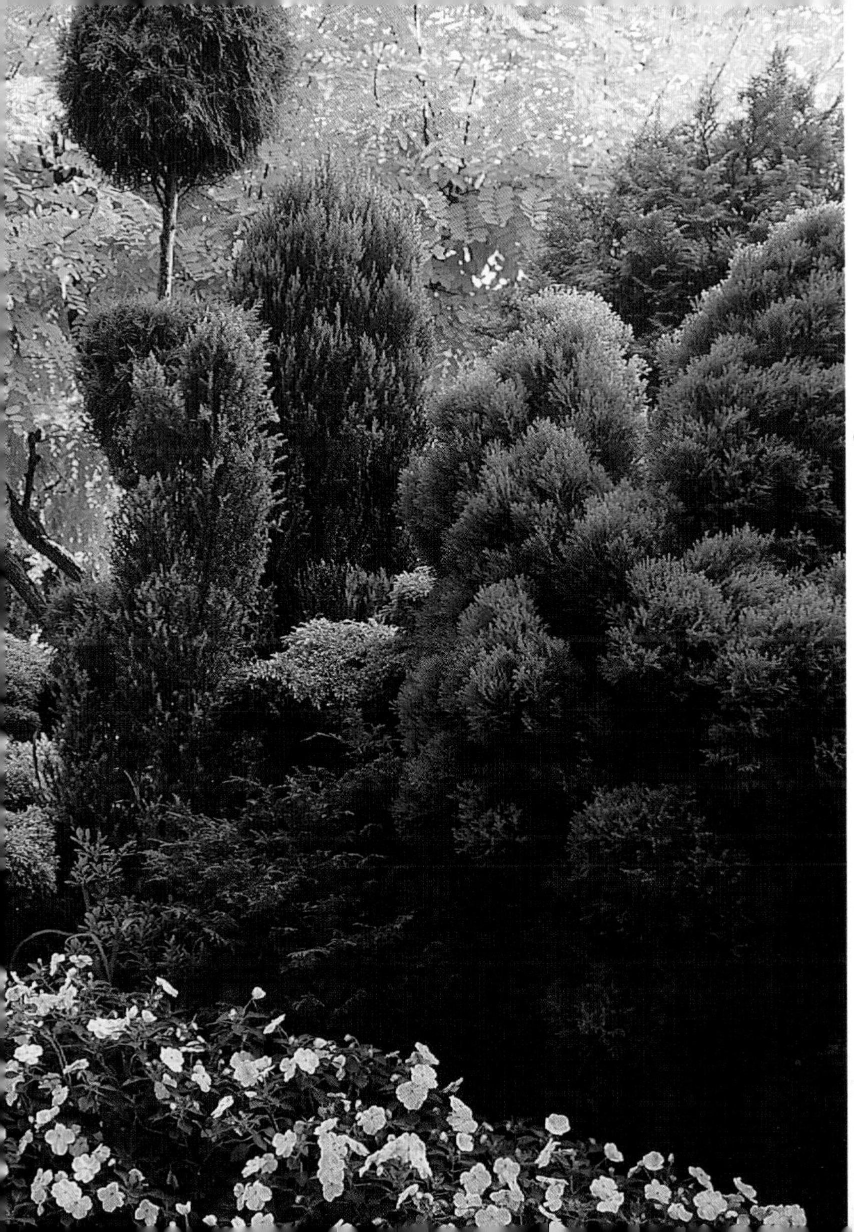

SHAPES AND HEDGES

Plants with interesting shapes bring wonderful symmetry and form to the garden. They offer all sorts of design possibilities. Their impact is immediate—a potted conifer makes a striking feature; a leafy hedge forms a green canvas for a spray of bright blooms; whimsical topiaries create interest and curiosity; and big balls of blue hydrangeas are showy companions for statuary.

Clipped and shaped evergreens make year-round features.
Previous pages: Pretty allium has naturally rounded blooms.

Some of these plants can be helped along with an occasional trim, others do it alone. Play up their geometric shapes by accentuating them in structured beds or teaming them with some garden ornaments. Or, use balls, buns or cones to contrast with irregularly shaped plants.

Most well-structured plants lend themselves to planting as hedges or screens. The best have dense growth,

The clipped and formal domes of azaleas make an elegant yet restrained feature in this Japanese-inspired garden.

small leaves and foliage to ground level. Many are evergreen, which means year-round foliage. In a cold climate, where many plants survive long winters by becoming dormant, a neatly trimmed evergreen hedge or topiary plant makes an attractive garden feature. Whatever the setting—cold, tropical, coastal or dry—there's a shapely plant that will make your garden special.

Some plants have naturally rounded or conical forms while others lend themselves to trimming into geometric shapes.

ALLIUM SPECIES
ORNAMENTAL ONION

Top: The round flower heads of ornamental onions offer pretty fluff balls in gorgeous pink. Above: *A. christophii* has fascinating flower heads arranged in spiralling balls.

Despite the onion tag in their name, ornamental alliums produce a wonderful array of flowers with bright colours and lots of character. The globular heads are made up of hundreds of star-like blooms in purple, pink or white tones. One of the most eye-catching ornamentals is *Allium giganteum*; it has dense, purple, violet or pink blooms which rise on stout, 1m (3 ft) stems. *A. aflatunense* is a large, summer-growing species that also produces dense, star-shaped blooms in purplish pink. Once flowering has finished, seed heads follow. The heads of *A. christophii* persist after the rest of the plant has disappeared into summer dormancy. This species makes an excellent dried flower. Ornamental alliums look spectacular mass-planted in a border, grown in a rockery or mixed with soft, silver-leaved or low-mounding plants.

GROWING NOTES

Alliums perform best in a cool to mild climate with well-drained soil and full sun. They flower in spring—some species lasting for 5–6 weeks. Bulbs of most species will spread and multiply and plants can also be grown from seed. All have an onion smell when the stems or leaves are bruised.

ARGYRANTHEMUM SPECIES
MARGUERITE DAISIES

Bright and cheery, daisies are a delight to have in any garden, especially the cottage style. While these fast-growing subshrubs thrive in most coastal areas, growing to 1 metre (3 ft), they do well in both hot and cold climates. They look wonderful mass-planted for a swathe of colour, highlighting a path or accenting a set of steps. They also grow well in pots. Daisies develop a pleasing, rounded shape, particularly when young. Many modern cultivars grow in a neat bun without any additional pruning. Use these compact balls as a centrepiece in a large urn or to give structure to a cottage-garden bed. Daisies are known for their simple, single white flowers but also come in pretty pink and yellow tones. Their forms vary, too. Many have contrasting centres, some have double flowers and others have centres comprising tiny petals.

GROWING NOTES

Excellent drainage and full sun spell success with the fast-growing daisy. Some varieties are sensitive to cold so choose with care in frosty districts. In very cold climates use daisies as annuals. Lightly shear after each wave of flowering.

There are more than 20,000 species in the daisy family and these easy-care beauties will grow in most climates. They work well in mass-plantings, garden beds, hanging baskets and as potted specimens.

ARGYRODERMA SPECIES (SYN. *LITHOPS* SPECIES)
LIVING STONES

Animal, vegetable or mineral? These living stones are succulents and one of the plant world's little curiosities.

The fascination with living stones is their striking resemblance to colourful stones. They're even more amazing when these 'pebbles' begin to bloom. The daisy-like flowers in yellow, purple, red or white, resemble those of the ice plant, a close relative. Living stones grow to about 2cm (1 inch) high so are a very useful groundcover in a succulent or cactus garden, particularly mingled with sand, quartz or pebbles. They can be grown in pots and make an interesting display for a windowsill or patio table. Children find them particularly appealing and what better way to introduce them to the wonderful world of plants?

GROWING NOTES

Living stones have very specific needs (they originally come from arid regions of South Africa). They must have excellent drainage and should never be overwatered. In particular, they need to be kept dry during winter when they are dormant. They may disappear to ground level at this stage. Living stones enjoy a sunny spot, but can get burnt in a very hot sun.

RHODODENDRON SPECIES
AZALEAS

Evergreen azaleas are handy plants—they offer plenty of colourful flowers each spring and their foliage is perfect for creating structure and interest all year round. These reliable plants can be clipped into balls, formed into hedges or trained into lollipop-style standards. And there are lots to choose from. The easiest to manage and train are the tall-growing varieties such as the white-flowered 'Alba Magnifica' (also sold as 'Alba Magna'). This variety also has a delightful fragrance. The small-leaved and small-flowered kurume azaleas, such as 'Kirin', also form neat flowering balls and hedges. Azaleas with naturally small, rounded shapes can be used as low border plants. For year-round colour, try the purple-leaved azalea 'Plumtastic'.

GROWING NOTES
Evergreen azaleas thrive in a temperate climate in slightly acid soil. In cold zones select deciduous species. Azaleas prefer filtered sun but become leggy and prone to pests if grown in deep shade. Azaleas have shallow roots so it's a good idea to give them a layer of organic mulch. The shallow root system also makes them ideally suited to containers.

With a little trimming and training, azaleas can be styled into compact formal shapes such as pretty floral balls or hedges.

BERBERIS SPECIES
BARBERRY

Naturally rounded barberry makes a handsome permanent barrier plant, and has seasonal interest in the form of spring flowers and autumn leaves.

Despite its naturally round and pleasing form, barberry is not a shrub that you want to get up close and personal with. Beneath that mound of neat leaves lurks a mass of sharp spines. With such thorny features, it makes an ideal barrier plant and quickly deters anyone who crosses its path. Barberry branches low from the ground to form a rounded ball to about 1.5–3 metres (5–10 ft) high and wide. In spring they are massed with tiny, usually yellow to orange flowers. These deciduous shrubs produce glorious foliage colour throughout autumn. Their berries, in shades of purple, blue and black, provide additional interest. During the winter, the barberry shrub becomes a network of twiggy branches. Some cultivars, such as *Berberis thunbergii* 'Atropurpurea', have burgundy-coloured leaves. For a compact barrier plant, try *B. thunbergii* 'Atropurpurea Nana'; its attractive bun-like shape grows to only 30–45 cm (12–18 inches) tall.

GROWING NOTES

Barberry is easy to grow and performs best in a cold to mild climate with sun and free-draining soil. Autumn colour is better in full sun. Prune after flowering to maintain a hedge.

BUXUS SPECIES
BOX

Formal hedging or imaginative topiary, the versatile and hardy box can easily be clipped into shapes that suit any garden design.

Box is the ideal hedging or topiary plant. Its neat and compact growth makes it a perfect candidate for clipping and shaping. And, as it's a slow-growing plant, it doesn't require trimming all that often. Whether you want to create a formal hedge, parterre or a whimsical topiary shape, this evergreen shrub will perform beautifully.

GROWING NOTES

Box withstands all adversities from shade and poor soils to a polluted city environment. However, all species are at their best in full sun. Common box (*Buxus sempervirens*) has small, neat, dark-green growth and a slightly acrid smell. Growing to around 1–1.8 metres (3–6 ft) tall, it can be easily maintained and suits a cool climate. The edging box, *B. sempervirens* 'Suffruticosa', which only grows to about 30 cm (12 inches), is a good choice for a dwarf hedge. Where conditions are warm and humid, Japanese box (*B. microphylla* var. *japonica*) is the better choice. It has rounded, glossy leaves, grows more quickly than the common box and lacks the acrid smell.

CUPRESSUS SEMPERVIRENS 'STRICTA'
ITALIAN CYPRESS

The bold and beautiful Italian cypress has an awesome presence. It shines in its native home, where its tall, conical shape forms a dark-green exclamation point in the landscape or against buildings. It is an ideal plant to introduce a Mediterranean feel, whether as one vertical accent plant, a pair or a row. This versatile plant also makes a tall, evergreen hedge and can be used to accentuate a wall or sculpture. Full-grown trees can reach 25 metres (75 ft) in height. For glorious golden colour, the Australian cultivar, *C. sempervirens* 'Swane's Golden', is a great choice. This slow-growing, columnar tree reaches about 4 metres (12 ft) in height. An impressive narrow form is 'Gracilis', which grows to about 4 metres (12 ft) high and 1 metre (3 ft) wide.

GROWING NOTES
Italian cypress grows well in cool to subtropical zones but prefers well-drained loam. Plants can be lightly clipped and shaped but don't cut into old wood. Golden forms are susceptible to foliage burn if exposed to hot or dry conditions.

'Swane's Golden' (above) has flecked, golden foliage that glows in the sun. *C. sempervirens* 'Stricta' (opposite) works well in a formal garden and looks majestic flanking the entrance to a property.

HEBE SPECIES
HEBE, VERONICA

If you're after a plant that's as neat as a pin and trouble-free, then pretty hebe will fit the bill. This naturally rounded, evergreen shrub features small spires of white, pink or mauve flowers that are abundant from autumn to early spring. The range of species and named varieties is enormous. Some forms have golden or variegated leaves and others, such as *Hebe buxifolia*, have small, fine, box-like foliage. They also range in size from compact plants under 1 metre (3 ft) high and wide to taller shrubs that are 2 metres (6 ft) high and wide. Hebes are particularly useful as an informal low hedge or as a foundation planting around a building or fence line. They can also be used to edge a driveway or path.

Hebes are grown for their naturally rounded shape but also produce attractive spires of long-lasting flowers in pastel shades.

GROWING NOTES
Hebes perform best in full sun and well-drained soil. They grow in cool to subtropical climates and are tolerant to both cold and drought. These hardy plants take salt spray and strong winds in their stride. Most species need little pruning or shaping as they naturally develop as a rounded bush.

HYDRANGEA MACROPHYLLA
MOPTOP HYDRANGEA

Hydrangeas put on a showy display in summer, producing large 'moptops' of flowers in gorgeous colours. These shade-loving plants are an ideal choice for mass-planting on the shady side of a building or wall. They also make an excellent specimen plant in a shrub border under deciduous trees or in containers. The flower heads are made up of masses of pink, blue or white flowers, which can persist into autumn. In cool gardens, ageing flowers develop green and pink tones. Some modern cultivars have variegated pink-and-white or blue-and-white flowers and are compact shrubs for gardens or pots. Older varieties may grow to 2–3 metres (6–10 ft) tall and wide.

GROWING NOTES

Success with hydrangeas lies in watering and mulching. These plants will wilt dramatically if deprived of water on hot days. Water plants deeply during hot spells and protect their root area with a generous layer of organic mulch. Flower colour reflects chemical conditions in the soil, with pink forms common in soil that contains lime and blue forms associated with acidic soils. Prune after flowering or in winter when plants are bare.

Give hydrangeas plenty of water in summer and they'll reward you with large balls of colourful blooms for months.

LAURUS NOBILIS
BAY

In ancient times the smooth, leathery leaves of the bay were fashioned into wreaths to celebrate athletic success or scholarly achievement. Today, the bay is more likely to be grown in a kitchen garden for its aromatic leaves. The bay grows into a large tree, up to 10–20 metres (30–60 ft) tall and about 9 metres (30 ft) wide. However, with regular clipping and pruning, it can be contained to the desired size and shape. Where space is confined, keep a clipped bay in a large tub where it will provide structure and form. Contrast the dark-green, stiff leaves with coloured-foliage shrubs and trees. Use bay as a centrepiece in a kitchen or herb garden.

The bay tree has a canopy of naturally dense foliage, making it ideal for clipping into a ball-shaped head.

GROWING NOTES
Any sunny to partially shaded spot in rich garden loam will suit a bay. Plants are best in a Mediterranean climate, with dry summers and moist winters. In areas with wet, humid summers, grow bays in containers with well-drained potting mix. Apply lime where soils or potting mixes are acidic.

LAVANDULA SPECIES
LAVENDER

French lavender's mauve flowers, grey-green foliage and naturally rounded shape make it an ideal low hedging plant. Opposite: Italian lavender.

Lovely lavender has been a favourite of gardeners since early Roman times, and with good reason. It brings colour, scent, form and texture to a garden. In its other life, this evergreen shrub produces an oil that has healing properties and its flowers are dried for potpourri and fragrant sachets. Lavender grows as a naturally rounded small to medium-sized shrub with grey-green to silver spiky leaves and tall stems of purple, mauve, pink, white or green flowers. Different species and varieties flower in different seasons. The summer-flowering English lavender (*Lavandula angustifolia*) is grown commercially for oil and flower production.

Use lavenders as a feature or mass them in a row for an informal hedge. For something a little different, consider using lavender bushes to hedge a vegetable garden or to surround a clothesline area. Lavenders are a popular choice for cottage gardens and are a big hit with bees when in bloom. The soft grey-greens or silver hues of the leaves are a foil for brightly coloured cottage-garden plants like poppies and daisies. The upright flower spikes also provide interest among more blousy flowering plants such as roses. Lavender is equally at home in Mediterranean or dry gardens, too.

Italian lavender (*L. stoechas*) is another star performer. It has a distinctive flower head that sports a pair of pink-purple ear-like petals on top of a column of deep purple flowers. There are many named and compact forms of this striking species, making it a good choice in a range of gardens. Italian lavender does well even in warm coastal climates. It begins flowering in winter, bringing colour to gardens over several months.

French lavender (*L. dentata*) is grown for its aromatic silver leaves and graceful flowers. It is adaptable to a wide range of climates and soils and will grow well in cool to temperate and coastal zones. It is not long-lived in humid or poorly drained areas. French lavender flowers in winter and spring.

Above: Mass-planted, lavender is magnificent. For striking contrast, grow it with colourful shrubs, annuals or perennials. Opposite: *L. stoechas* is a mass of purple bloom from late winter.

GROWING NOTES

Lavenders need full sun, good air circulation and excellent soil drainage. They also benefit from added lime. They thrive in cool to temperate climates, but do not like poorly drained soils or humidity. In hot, humid climates they may be grown as annuals but last several years in cool, dry regions. Prune plants after flowering to maintain a compact shape.

LIGUSTRUM SPECIES
PRIVET

In some areas privet can become an invasive weed. But, properly managed and tamed with a pair of shears, it is one of the best choices available in temperate gardens for a long-lived, formal hedge or topiary plant. Unpruned privet can grow to 4 metres (12 ft) in height and produces strongly scented flowers in spring and masses of black fruits. Birds feast on the berries, freely spreading the seeds as they go. Several species of privet are classified as weeds in parts of Australia, New Zealand and the United States. Of the many ornamental privets it is the golden variety, *Ligustrum ovalifolium* 'Aureum', that is appealing as a hedge. It can be used in a mixed planting or to provide a colour contrast with mature trees and shrubs.

Fast-growing and easy-care, privets can be trimmed into handsome hedges in colours of bright green and gold.

GROWING NOTES

Privet is tolerant of a wide range of growing conditions, but is seen at its best in moist, well-nourished soil. If growing a golden variegated form, remove the green shoots to retain the overall golden form and grow in full sun.

LONICERA NITIDA
BOX HONEYSUCKLE

Box honeysuckle is a very effective hedging or topiary plant. Its small leaves and dense, twiggy habit make it ideal to clip and train. You can maintain it as a small, leafy hedge to 50 cm (20 inches) tall, along a path or low wall, or use it as a freestanding hedge, reaching to 1–2 metres (3–6 ft) in height. It can also be fashioned into a myriad of topiary shapes such as balls, spires or even animal forms. Box honeysuckle has small cream flowers in spring, which do not stand out among the mass of leaves. For vibrant foliage contrast, the golden variegated form, 'Aurea', works a treat.

The box honeysuckle has tiny, dense leaves that are easily clipped into a formal hedge. Its rapid growth ensures a quick result.

GROWING NOTES
The evergreen box honeysuckle can withstand hard or frequent clipping. It tolerates sun or shade and will grow in a wide range of soils. It performs best in cool to temperate climates but will tolerate subtropical zones. Although box honeysuckle produces purple berries, its fruit are rarely seen in cultivation, which means this plant is unlikely to become invasive in natural bushland areas or surrounding gardens.

MURRAYA PANICULATA
ORANGE JESSAMINE

Murraya is a superb shrub with fragrant flowers and dense, evergreen foliage. It is an excellent choice for a privacy screen between neighbouring properties or as a formal or informal hedge along a boundary. Alternatively, use it to divide gardens into separate sections or to wrap around a swimming pool. Unpruned orange jessamine will grow to a shrubby tree 3 metres (10 ft) high and 2 metres (6 ft) wide but, with regular clipping from planting, can be maintained as a hedge about 1.5–2 metres (4–6 ft) high. Its foliage extends right to the base of the plant. This plant works well as one part of a stepped or tiered hedge. Use it for height teamed with lower-growing shrubs like box, gardenia or box honeysuckle. Its deep-green leaves contrast well with gold or light-green foliage.

Although widely grown as a hedge, Murraya paniculata can be grown to form a freestanding shrub and clipped into decorative shape. Creamy white, perfumed flowers appear in spring.

GROWING NOTES
Murraya grows in sun or shade but flowering is reduced in shady areas. It grows best in a warm, frost-free climate with regular deep watering, particularly in spring and summer.

NANDINA DOMESTICA
DWARF NANDINA, JAPANESE SACRED BAMBOO

The dwarf nandina, *Nandina domestica* 'Nana', is a top-performing ornamental shrub. This low-growing beauty provides vibrant winter colour, is hardy and requires little maintenance. It forms a naturally small, rounded bun, growing to 30 cm (12 inches) high, with evergreen leaves turning flaming red during the winter months. The red tones provide a cheerful note amid winter deciduous plants and contrast well against the evergreen foliage. It can be used to edge a path or garden bed, or as a feature in a Japanese-inspired garden. For a taller plant, select the Japanese sacred bamboo or the cultivar 'Gulf Stream'. This plant grows to 1 metre (3 ft) tall and wide with gold to red winter colours.

GROWING NOTES

Although the dwarf nandina is tolerant of harsh conditions, it grows best with full sun and ample water, particularly in summer. Soil should be well drained and rich in organic matter. Plants need little trimming or shaping. Foliage colour is accentuated by cold winter conditions.

Opposite: The taller Japanese sacred bamboo produces bright red berries on plants that reach to 1–2 metres (3–6 ft) high. Below: The colours and rounded shape of the dwarf nandina make it an excellent choice for a low garden border.

PARODIA SPECIES (SYN. *NOTOCACTUS* SPECIES)
BALL CACTUS

The easily grown ball cactus has loads of character. It forms colonies of ribbed, spiny spheres, each topped with a cute little flower.

A long with their fascinating shapes ball cacti bring an interesting array of textures and colours to the garden. Most species have a distinctive round or oval shape, strong ribbing and prominent spines. Particularly dramatic is *P. magnifica* (syn. *Notocactus magnificus*), which has a blue-green skin and strongly accentuated ribs lined with spines. Ball cacti (which includes *Parodia* and the closely related genera *Notocactus* and *Eriocactus*) can be grown in a cactus garden, where they form slow-growing colonies. They will also thrive in pots. Plants willingly flower and are easy to grow. The boldly coloured yellow or pink flowers emerge from the top of the spiky balls. Their glossy flat petals contrast with the surrounding spines. For a geometric effect, combine the round forms of ball cactus with gravel and small, rounded pebbles.

GROWING NOTES

Ball cacti, like most of their prickly relatives, need full sun and excellent drainage. Use a gravel mix when planting in containers. Some species are sensitive to frost and need protection in winter. Water well during the summer months.

PHOTINIA SPECIES
PHOTINIA

Photonias are tough, long-lived plants that love to be whipped into shape with shears. Indeed, most respond with a bold show of crimson new leaf growth that lights up the landscape. They are seen at their peak in cool to cold climates or in inland areas where winters are cold. The strong red foliage tones contrast superbly with green or golden trees and shrubs. Photinia is the perfect plant for defining a boundary or screening sections of a garden. For a stylish and colourful presentation, grow a photinia hedge around a rose garden. The popular hedging photinia, *Photinia glabra* 'Rubens', has flushes of crimson in its new growth.

While photinias produce a mass of creamy flowers in spring, it is their distinctive red new growth and dense evergreen foliage that make them perfect specimens for hedging.

GROWING NOTES
While photinias grow in a wide range of soils and climates, they are at their best in rich, well-drained soils in full sun. To maintain their deep-red leaf colours, plants should be well watered and trimmed occasionally through the warm months. Photinias need to be pruned heavily in winter.

PICEA ABIES
NORWAY SPRUCE

Norway spruce is the stuff of postcards with its lustrous dark-green leaves and Christmas-tree shape. This magnificent tree is best grown in cool climates where its form is slender and conical. In these conditions, it can grow to 20–45 metres (60–135 ft) tall. In smaller gardens, choose one of the dwarf forms with a natural conical shape. They need no pruning to maintain their appealing geometric forms and are slow-growing. Some dwarf varieties are under 1 metre (3 ft) tall while others, like 'Compacta', grow slowly to 3 metres (10 ft). Make the most of their conical shapes and position them in key areas in the garden such as a rockery, along a driveway or in pots. Larger trees look best in a park-like garden surrounded by deciduous spreading trees such as golden elms.

Dwarf conifers add another dimension to this garden of many colours. This compact form grows naturally into a conical shape so there's no need to prune.

GROWING NOTES
Norway spruce is very much a cool-climate tree. It needs rich, deep, neutral to acid soil, regular watering and protection from the hot summer sun and harsh winds.

PRUNUS LAUROCERASUS
CHERRY LAUREL

Not just a pretty face, the evergreen cherry laurel can be used to define a boundary, as a foil for winter deciduous trees, or to provide shelter from strong winter winds.

Cherry laurel makes an imposing hedge of dark-green glossy leaves. This cool-climate shrub will grow into a loose tree to 3 metres (10 ft) tall, if it is not pruned. As a formal, evergreen hedge it provides structure in a garden. It can be kept to a neat 1 metre (3 ft) high or allowed to grow taller. This plant makes a good windbreak for an exposed corner or use it as a dark-green background for ornamental plants. It contrasts well with dainty deciduous trees such as Japanese maples. Although mainly thought of as a leafy hedge, cherry laurel does flower. The perfumed, white flowers are followed by tiny, red, cherry-like fruit. Enjoy the blooms without the fruit by pruning after the spring flowers have passed.

GROWING NOTES

Cherry laurel grows well in sun or partial shade in a cool to cold climate with reliable moisture. One of the toughest of evergreens, it is a very long-lived plant where conditions are ideal. In warmer areas it needs ample water and rich soil.

ROBINIA PSEUDOACACIA 'UMBRACULIFERA'
MOP TOP, MOPHEAD ACACIA

Robinias have a natural beauty—dense, textured foliage in shades of soft green and long slender trunks. However, they look stunning with a little clever grafting. Enter the mop top. Here, a naturally rounded cultivar can be transformed into a lollipop shape—a tall, straight trunk and a round head of fern-like leaves. While most robinias have wisteria-like flowers, the mop top rarely blooms. It has the added benefit of being thornless. This is an ideal tree for a small courtyard or narrow boundary and is quite at home in a formal garden. It brings form and interest, especially when used as a living umbrella. Its height varies, depending on the height of the stem when the graft is made, but trees can reach 5 metres (15 ft) high with the same spread.

GROWING NOTES
Mop tops thrive in cold to subtropical zones. Avoid unwanted suckers by keeping plants well watered. Do not damage the trunk or roots when digging or trimming lawns.

A living shadecloth, the mop top brings a canopy of lush green foliage to a courtyard or patio.

SANTOLINA CHAMAECYPARISSUS
COTTON LAVENDER

Beautiful in more ways than one, cotton lavender makes a stylish edging plant. Its lovely silver-grey leaves are aromatic when crushed, emitting a lavender-like fragrance.

Cotton lavender is a wonderful little shrub for lots of reasons. It has a naturally dense, rounded shape, bears pretty summer flowers and has aromatic silver-grey leaves. This hardy plant grows to about 30–45 cm (12–18 inches) tall and up to 1 metre (3 ft) wide. It can be clipped to maintain a regular shape. In summer the plant bursts into bloom with heads of golden flowers. If these are at odds with your garden scheme, trim the plant in late spring to early summer and they're gone. It performs well as an informal silver-grey border or as a plant that softly laps the edges of paths or steps. A versatile plant, it can be teamed with flowery cottage favourites or sculptural succulents. It is also an excellent alternative to lavender for gardens in humid climates.

GROWING NOTES

Cotton lavender is a Mediterranean plant that relishes long, hot summers. It is drought hardy when established. In areas with moist or humid summers, plant it in well-drained soil.

SPIRAEA CANTONIENSIS
MAY, REEVES' SPIRAEA

The clusters of tiny, white, rose-like flowers of *Spiraea cantoniensis* brighten up gardens in early spring. It is equally beautiful as a single feature specimen or among mixed shrubs.

For big balls of gorgeous white flowers, enlist a shrub or two of may. This deciduous plant has its main flush of showy blooms in spring. Even when may's not in flower, it forms a pleasantly rounded shape. For an elegant formal look, simply shear over the plant after flowering to bring it into a smooth ball shape. Expect plants to grow to around 1.8 metres (6 ft) tall and nearly as wide. There are many species and named varieties of may to suit most situations. Where a small, rounded shrub is needed, look for compact cultivars of Japanese spiraea such as the pink-flowered 'Anthony Waterer', the bronze- to golden-leaved 'Goldflame' or the petite 'Nana' at only 45 cm (18 inches) high. May is striking as a feature plant, informal hedge or in a mixed-shrub border.

GROWING NOTES

May thrives in a temperate climate. It likes moist, well-drained soils but once established, it becomes drought tolerant. It needs to be sheltered from the full heat of the afternoon sun.

TAXUS BACCATA
YEW

Yews are long-lived evergreens that are tailor-made for hedging and topiary. They may look like flowering shrubs, but they are conifers. These slow-growing trees are suited to cold climates where they are often used as a dense screen to protect flower gardens against harsh winter winds. There is an affinity between yew and garden ornaments. The neat, dark-green, dense growth of yew forms a powerful foil for marble or stone statues. To bring a flash of colour, position an urn in front of a yew hedge and plant it with a cold-tolerant, variegated plant. Yews can also be trained in a variety of topiary shapes, including cones, spirals, balls and obelisks. Unpruned yew hedges grow to around 15 metres (45 ft) tall but are mostly maintained at 2–3 metres (6–10 ft).

With its densely packed spirals of needle-like leaves, yews can be clipped and trained into formal hedges.

GROWING NOTES

Yew is a plant for cool climates. In hot or dry weather, make sure plants are kept well watered. It grows best when it is lightly but frequently pruned. However, an overgrown yew hedge can be pruned severely and allowed to regenerate. The red berries found on yews are poisonous.

THUJA SPECIES
THUJA

The vertical leaflets of many thujas are arranged like pages in a book, giving these dense conifers the common name of bookleaf.

Some of the small, slow-growing thujas produce the best shapes of all garden conifers. They can be flat and spreading, round and bun-shaped, or form a compact pyramidal shape like the widely grown *T. occidentalis* 'Smaragd'. Growing to around 1.8 metres (6 ft) tall, 'Smaragd' is an excellent choice for a dense, slow-growing hedge. Thuja's distinctive feathery foliage comes in glorious iridescent green or gold colours that can intensify in winter. The larger and fast-growing western red cedar (*T. plicata*) grows to 24 metres (80 ft) in cultivation.

GROWING NOTES

Thujas will thrive in cool to temperate climates. Although adaptable to a range of soils, plants grow best in well-drained soils. Drought tolerant once established, thujas need additional watering in hot or dry weather. Protect golden forms from damage by hot winds and strong afternoon sun.

topiary

Topiary is simply the art of clipping and training plants into decorative forms. It can turn plants into living sculptures. This ancient artform traces its origins back to the first century AD in Rome. Today, it remains a popular form of garden design and is seen in a wide range of landscapes. Topiary can be as tall as a conifer, as small as a ball of box and as quaint as a set of animal shapes.

Topiary uses plants as architecture (hedging) and as sculpture (ornamental shapes). Hedging is topiary in its simplest form; it is a living wall that provides containment, privacy and shelter. Geometrical shapes such as hedges, cones and standards (shrubs grown on a single stem with their lower branches removed) are similar to hedging in that they form a backbone to the design no matter what the season. They also add a sense of order and permanence to the garden. By contrast, where topiary is used to create living ornaments, such as animal shapes, they add character and whimsy to a garden.

The easiest topiaries to start with are the simple geometric shapes such as pillars, balls, cubes, cones and pyramids. Position these shapes where they'll have maximum impact; that is, as punctuation points in the garden. Use them to mark corners, sit them along a path or hedge, or in pairs flanking an entry point. Such shapes can also work powerfully in pots. For a dramatic arrangement, line a set of steps with terracotta pots, each containing a simple ball of *Buxus* (box). Or, consider a stately pair of sweet bay spires flanking the front door. Some plants, such as conifers, naturally form cone, pillar and candle shapes, requiring little pruning to enhance their shape. For balls and cubes, box is best, but others such as *Myrtus*, *Berberis*, *Lonicera*, *Syzygium* and *Euonymous* can be used.

Previous page: Green vertical elements have greater impact when contrasted with rounded beds of bright blooms. Clockwise from top left: Standards bring formality to the garden; this golden conifer adds a new twist; parterre can be used to great effect with a mix of different foliage; and low hedges and tall pyramids give depth and dimension.

The ultimate topiaries are plants clipped into animal shapes, forming living sculptures. Tightly clipped box hedging makes a perfect surround to the focal point, with counterpoints of small cones and balls.

Standards are perhaps the most widely known form of topiary. They form the classic lollipop shape or ball-on-a-stick. Standards do not increase in height significantly, but the heads grow bigger and thicker. There's a wide range of plants that can be used for standards. Those that flower include roses, camellias, azaleas, fuchsias, gardenias, oleander and duranta. Fruiting standards include cumquats, olives, lillypillies and crabapples. For crisp green globes, conifers, box, ficus and sweet bay are popular. Standards are often used as feature specimens in decorative pots, particularly as a pair flanking a doorway. A single standard makes a strong centrepiece for a geometrically designed garden, while rows of standards can line a formal pathway or lead the eye through the garden.

The art of topiary is limited only by your imagination. Like living sculptures, topiaries have been fashioned into extraordinary shapes. There are menageries of animals—from elephants to peacocks—fantasy characters, crenellated walls, steam trains, entire chess sets and even a foxhunting scene. Most of these shapes are created by clipping long-living plants such as yew and box; this usually takes several years. Topiarists use a metal framework that outlines the desired shape and

provides a guide for clipping. A faster and easier method is to use a wire-mesh frame set in a pot with a climbing plant to grow over it. Plants that work well for this method are maidenhair creeper (*Muehlenbeckia*), ivy and creeping fig (*Ficus pumila*).

Topiary also includes plants grown to form patterns on the ground, such as mazes, knot gardens and parterre gardens. Knot gardens are designed to reflect the intricate patterns of embroidery and feature low, tightly clipped hedges. Similarly, parterre gardens, originally designed to be viewed from the upper floors of a chateau, feature scroll patterns based on leaf and flower motifs. The designs are set against a contrasting background of coloured gravel, with compartments formed by the patterns that are sometimes infilled with flowers or vegetables. Mazes are a fascinating form of topiary and can be made from any durable hedging plant, depending on the height desired for the walls.

Successful topiary depends on regular clipping to keep the form densely filled and sharply outlined. The more you prune, the thicker the plant becomes. Slow-growing species in cool climates may need clipping only twice a year. By contrast, the

Clockwise from top left: Clipped plants can be used to form a variety of patterns and shapes to add structure to the garden; mazes are an ancient form of topiary and have a special fascination; use blocks of hedging to echo built structures; and a zigzag pattern creates interesting compartments for planting.

fast-growing plants in warm areas may need tidying every six weeks during the growing months. You'll need either single-handed shears or a small pair of hedging shears. For detailed trimming, use a good pair of secateurs. When working on larger items, such as pillars, obelisks and small hedges, hedging shears with telescopic handles are ideal. Powered hedge-trimmers, whether electric, battery-operated or with a petrol engine, will save hours of labour on large and long hedges. Remember to wear protective clothing and goggles when using power tools. For a professional finish, use good-quality tools that are well sharpened.

Some gardeners have a good eye for clipping a shape accurately. Others will find a template or former useful. A former is a wooden frame with wire-mesh sides that is slipped over the plant when pruning. It is very useful for ensuring uniformity in a series of squares or pyramids. For perfectly straight hedges, use a stringline as a guide. To ease the job of tidying up afterwards, lay an old sheet on the ground around the plants before trimming.

Simple geometric shapes, such as balls and cones, become important structural elements when strategically placed in the garden landscape.

The trend to favour foliage plants is on the increase, and with good reason. Unlike traditional flowering plants, which have a brief showy period and then little to offer for the rest of the year, foliage plants provide colour, texture and form, month after month—and sometimes produce flowers as a bonus. Also, there is a wide range of foliage plants to choose from, with many

Foliage plants are perfect partners for water features. Use a mix of shapes, sizes and colours to create a jungle look. Previous pages: Many beautiful foliage plants are shade lovers that add rich texture to the area under trees.

species suited to cold climates. With such variety, a tropical-look garden can be achieved indoors or out.

There's a rich palette of colours on offer, too—bold, bright and soft—in stripes, spots, splashes and speckles.

Lush and coloured foliage evokes the wonderfully exotic and tropical nature of gardens. So wherever you create your little patch of paradise, you'll be well rewarded.

Bromeliads contribute both foliage colour and interesting form. Here, a collection is backed by the leopard plant. Following pages: For the lushest foliage effects, plant densely, and mix different foliage textures and colours.

ACALYPHA WILKESIANA AND CULTIVARS
FIJIAN FIRE PLANT

If vibrant, lively colour is your desire, the Fijian fire plant is a must-have, and you'll want to collect several of its varieties. The large, glossy leaves can be bronze to burgundy to pink, or perhaps lime-green and gold, and many are edged or splashed with contrasting colours. The overall effect simply glows. Fijian fire plant is a large and rounded shrub that grows to a height and spread of around 3 metres (10 ft). It makes a fabulous informal hedge or striking fill-in plant or can be featured as an accent specimen. The flowers are unusual bronze-red tassels, produced in summer and autumn, but they are not especially showy.

The beautifully coloured and patterned leaves of Fijian fire plants have great impact in a foliage garden. These long-lived perennials are also fast growing.

GROWING NOTES

A native of the Pacific Islands, Fijian fire plant needs a warm, frost-free position, preferably in subtropical and tropical regions. The foliage colour is brightest when in full sun, but it will cope with semi-shade. It can be grown in coastal gardens as long as it's not directly exposed to salt winds. A rich, well-drained soil is best, with ample water in summer.

ACANTHUS MOLLIS
BEAR'S BREECHES, OYSTER PLANT

The handsome, glossy, green leaves of bear's breeches can bring a tropical feel to both warm- and cool-climate gardens. Each leaf can be up to 60 cm (24 inches) long and nearly as wide. In spring and early summer, very tall flower spikes bear white-and-purple, oyster-shaped flowers. After flowering, the plant may die back before shooting again almost immediately. Bear's breeches forms large spreading clumps and is most effective when used in massed plantings. It tolerates shade, which makes it a handy groundcover to grow under trees or in clumps as an understorey plant. It is also useful as a border along a driveway or as a screen in front of a low wall.

GROWING NOTES
Bear's breeches is frost hardy, and grows in full sun or shade. Without moisture, or in hot weather, the leaves may wilt but recover quickly when given water. It can stand some waterlogging but gives its best in a rich, well-drained soil.

Acanthus mollis is effective when used for large banks of sculptural foliage. Lining a set of steps is a great way to show off its majestic leaves and pretty blooms.

ALOCASIA SPECIES
ELEPHANT'S EAR, CUNJEVOI

The structure of these very large, soft leaves is simple, yet dramatic. Elephant's ear is related to taro, but unlike its cousin, it is not an edible plant.

There's no mystery as to why elephant's ears are so named, especially when you see the huge leaves flapping gently in a light breeze. Held aloft on fleshy stems the soft, heart- or arrowhead-shaped leaves can be up to 1 metre (3 ft) long. They arise from a swollen rhizome or rootstock, as do the arum-type flowers. These are not very showy, but have a light fragrance. The berry-like fruits that form after flowering ripen to a bright orange-red colour. Some species have silver veining or distinctive purplish markings on the leaves. Use elephant's ear for large clumps of lush foliage to underplant palms or rainforest trees. It makes a strong statement in a large container and can also be grown indoors.

GROWING NOTES
Indigenous to tropical southeast Asia, elephant's ear loves warmth and humidity. It thrives in glasshouses and conservatories and requires little attention other than removal of old leaves. Give it shade or filtered light, and a rich, moist soil with plenty of organic matter and ample water.

ALPINIA SPECIES
ORNAMENTAL GINGER

With wildly vibrant, glowing flowers sprouting from lush foliage, the ornamental gingers have a lot to offer a tropical-style garden. *Alpinia purpurata*, red ginger, produces showy clusters of scarlet-red for most of the year and forms an erect clump to 2 metres (6 ft) tall. Shell ginger, *A. zerumbet*, bears pretty drooping sprays of flowers that start as ivory-coloured, satiny buds and blossom into bright yellow-and-red blooms. This clump-forming perennial grows to 3 metres (9 ft) high and wide. Gingers grow rapidly from a fleshy rhizome and are usually evergreen. Most have glossy, deep-green leaves but there are variegated forms available. The Thai spice, galangal, comes from the root of *A. galanga*. While the ornamental gingers are edible, they are not grown for this purpose, unlike *A. galanga*.

GROWING NOTES

Although ornamental gingers are frost tender, they can tolerate temperatures to around 5°C (41°F) if the summers are warm and humid. They like a semi-shaded position and permanently moist soil that's enriched with organic matter.

Ornamental gingers need a warm and moist position to bear their showy blooms. They do not die back and can be used in the garden like a shrub.

ANTHURIUM SPECIES
FLAMINGO FLOWER

The exotic and alluring flamingo flowers are produced for most of the year in favourable conditions, set against dark, decorative foliage.

Flamingo flowers are good value—they're strikingly beautiful in bloom and have attractive foliage when they're not. With their vivid colours and exotic looks, these tropical perennials make both spectacular cut flowers and indoor plants. The large spathes of the flamingo flower come in a range of gorgeous colours, including brilliant red, shades of pink, orange or white, and are often so glossy they appear to be varnished. The leathery, dark-green leaves are heart- or arrowhead-shaped. The blooms last for several weeks.

GROWING NOTES

In tropical areas, flamingo flowers are easy to grow, preferring some shelter from the sun and wind, and a rich, well-drained moist soil. In areas where the temperature falls below 16°C (60°F), or if humidity is low, they should be grown in a glasshouse or indoors. They need bright light, steady warmth and high humidity. Divide or repot them every few years, as the creeping rhizome will spread over the side of the pot.

ARDISIA CRENATA
CORAL BERRY

Plants that provide winter colour are always valued, and when they perform in shady areas, they are doubly welcome. The coral berry is one such plant. It bears masses of tiny, white flowers in summer which produce brilliant red, lustrous berries that persist in generous clusters through the winter months. Its deep-green, glossy leaves make a perfect backdrop to the display, with attractively crimped edges. Coral berry grows to 1 metre (3 ft) high, usually on a series of single stems. Use it as a feature in shady gardens, where a small group will have more impact than a single plant. It is also suitable as a pot plant for outdoors or indoors in a well-lit position.

With its winter display of shiny leaves and bright red berries, coral berry looks a lot like holly. A compact shrub, it is suitable for small gardens and as a potted indoor plant.

GROWING NOTES
At home in tropical and subtropical climates, coral berry will grow in temperate areas with light frosts. It prefers a shaded to semi-shaded position and soil enriched with organic matter, but will also tolerate other soil types. Keep well watered in summer and protect from drying winds. Pinch out the tips regularly to promote a bushier plant.

ASPIDISTRA ELATIOR
CAST-IRON PLANT

This underrated, handsome foliage plant got its common name from its ability to withstand extremely low light and neglect. It was the houseplant of choice in dark Victorian houses where it would survive even when coated with dust. The broad, blade-like leaves are up to 70 cm (30 inches) long, dark-green and curving gracefully at the tips. They form an upright clump that spreads slowly by underground rhizomes. The cast-iron plant is at its best when mass-planted in difficult, shady spots in the garden, and suits jungle and formal styles. The sweetly scented, bell-shaped flowers are cream to purple, but are seen only on mature plants at ground level. A variegated cultivar has irregular cream stripes along the leaves.

GROWING NOTES

The cast-iron plant originates from China. While it will grow in any well-drained soil, it gives its best in fertile, humus-rich soils. It needs protection from the sun, but it survives in cool and dark rooms and can live for long periods without water. It also tolerates moderate frosts.

The ultimate houseplant for non-gardeners, the cast-iron plant is one tough cookie—it can cope with low light and can tolerate long periods without water.

AUCUBA JAPONICA CULTIVARS
GOLD-DUST SHRUB, JAPANESE LAUREL

Aucuba japonica is a tough, resilient plant that copes in most conditions. But given a little care it will reward with handsome luxuriant growth.

Plants with foliage as exotic as this are often tender and tricky to grow, but the gold-dust shrub is a garden stalwart. The thick and glossy leaves have toothed edges and are liberally splashed, spotted or streaked with shiny gold. This slow-growing evergreen shrub grows to 3 metres (10 ft) high. Dense and luxuriant, it can be used as an informal hedge or screening shrub, or to bring light to a dark corner of the garden. It is also suitable as a container plant and can be grown indoors in bright light. The flowers are inconspicuous, but red berries may form if both male and female plants are present.

GROWING NOTES

The gold-dust plant is tough enough to withstand frost, neglect and heavy shade. Of course, it will perform better if given kinder treatment. It prefers a well-drained soil enriched with organic matter and needs to be well watered and mulched. Dappled light, or a position with morning sun, will ensure the leaves won't get scorched by the sun.

BERGENIA CORDIFOLIA
BERGENIA, SAXIFRAGE

A groundcover plant with bold foliage texture is a useful addition to shady gardens, but when it has beautiful blooms as well, it's a winner. This evergreen perennial has leathery, rounded leaves up to 25 cm (10 inches) in diameter, forming clumps that spread. The clusters of rose-pink flowers are delightfully fragrant, carried just above the foliage on fleshy stalks. They are especially valued for appearances in late winter and make excellent cut flowers. In cold areas, flowering is delayed until early spring. Mass-plant bergenia as a groundcover in woodland areas, or use it to edge a shady path or even clump it around a feature tree. Some cultivars have white, pale pink or crimson blooms.

Long-flowering and with a sweet, honey fragrance, pretty bergenia is an easy-care groundcover plant that deserves to be more widely grown.

GROWING NOTES

Bergenia grows in most soil types, as long as it has plenty of organic matter such as leaf mould or compost. It prefers a cool, moist and shaded position but can withstand sun and exposure as long as it is watered. Divide every few years and keep watch for snails and slugs.

CALADIUM SPECIES AND CULTIVARS
ANGEL WINGS

Few plants have such gorgeous colours displayed on their leaves as the aptly named angel wings. The leaves are also paper thin, showing the delicate tracery of veins in colours of pink, red, green and white. There are hundreds of cultivars, grown principally as indoor and conservatory plants, featuring intricate markings and multiple colour combinations. The arrowhead-shaped leaves can be as small as 2.5 cm (1 inch) long while the taller varieties grow in clumps that reach a height of 60 cm (24 inches). Angel wings grow from a tuber that is dormant in the dry season or in colder temperatures. The typical arum flowers do not compete with the exquisite leaves.

While the exquisitely patterned angel wings are suited to warm climates, you can still have the pleasure of their company if you grow them in a conservatory or glasshouse.

GROWING NOTES
At home in the tropics and subtropics, angel wings need a minimum temperature of 12°C (55°F) and high humidity. They like a moist, slightly shaded position with wind protection and a very rich but freely drained soil. Indoors, they need bright but not direct light and increased humidity from regular misting during the growing period. In cold climates, lift the tubers over winter and replant in spring.

CALATHEA SPECIES

PEACOCK OR ZEBRA PLANT

The boldly patterned leaves of the peacock plant make it a popular choice in a tropical garden or as an indoor attraction.

The wonderful peacock plant displays its finery all year round, making it a highly desirable foliage plant. Bold and exotic markings are its hallmark and, given the right climate, it makes an exciting contribution to shaded courtyards and lush foliage gardens. There are more than 300 species with patterned leaves in shades of green, cream, burgundy, pink and brown, often purplish on the undersides. Some are striped, others spotted, blotched or scalloped. They range in height from 20 cm (8 inches) to 2 metres (6 ft) and spread by underground rhizomes. The flowers range from a showy, torch-like cluster to small insignificant blooms.

GROWING NOTES

In the tropics and subtropics, peacock plants are happy growing outdoors and can cope with temperatures as low as 5°C (41°F). They need a sheltered, semi-shaded position and excellent drainage. Indoors, they tolerate fairly low light levels, but need bright light in order to flower. Good performers include *C. zebrina*, with large green-and-chocolate striped leaves, and *C. makoyana*, with classic, peacock-patterned leaves.

CANNA SPECIES AND CULTIVARS
INDIAN SHOT

In warm climates, cannas are such reliable plants they are sometimes dismissed as being a bit common. But, with their wonderful range of flower colours and new cultivars featuring multi-hued leaves, they should not be overlooked. Cannas grow in statuesque clumps up to 2.4 metres (8 ft) high with large, lush leaves and showy flowers. Related to gingers, the fleshy stems arise from a knobbly rhizome that is edible in some species. Foliage colour ranges from bright green to bronze or reddish, and more recent cultivars boast fine bronze, orange, cream and green stripes, which are dazzling. Flower colours range from flaming red, orange and apricot to yellow, pink and cream. Some varieties have spotted and bicolour flowers that are particularly alluring. When they flower, a seed capsule forms; it contains very hard, round, black seeds that resemble shotgun pellets, hence the plant's common name.

Cannas are big, bold and joyous, contributing bright colours and lush foliage in return for very little care and attention.

With cannas, the bigger the mass, the better the impact. These easy-care beauties come in a range of sizes and dazzling colours to suit any garden.

Cannas are not solo performers—their best impact is in large masses. They can fill a whole bed on their own, or be mixed in small groups among other plants in a border. Use them to colonize difficult, damp areas as long as they get some sun. Cannas come in a wide range of colours and sizes.

GROWING NOTES

Native to South America, cannas thrive in tropical and subtropical climates where they will flower all year. In warm temperate climates, they are cut to the ground in early winter; in colder areas, the rhizomes need mulching or lifting in autumn to prevent them from freezing. Cannas love sun and water, and will soak up water in wet areas. They are not fussy about soil type, but respond well to complete fertilizer in spring.

CODIAEUM VARIEGATUM VAR. *PICTUM*
CROTON

Very few plants can match the magnificent croton in the colour stakes. It's hard to imagine more brightly coloured foliage: splashed, spotted and striped in a hot and riotous mix of red, orange, yellow, green, white, bronze and pink. Forming small shrubs from about 1 metre (3 ft) to 2.5 metres (8 ft) in height, they are equally flamboyant in their leaf shape. These may be long and narrow, broadly oval or variously lobed, sometimes with twisted or wavy edges. In comparison, the tiny yellowish flowers are quite insignificant. Use crotons for brilliant colour, mass-planted or as an informal hedge, or as accent plants. They are also popular houseplants.

Dynamic crotons give their best display in warm-climate areas. Named croton cultivars are available for warm-climate gardens or as indoor plants in a range of glorious colours.

GROWING NOTES

Crotons are strictly for tropical and subtropical areas, where winter temperatures do not fall below 15°C (60°F). Full sun is needed to achieve the most intense colours, although they will grow in dappled shade. Give them a well-drained soil, rich in organic matter, with regular water and fertilizer. Indoors, provide a brightly lit position, avoiding any cold spots, and reduce watering during the winter months.

CORDYLINE FRUTICOSA AND CULTIVARS
TI, HAWAIIAN GOOD LUCK PLANT

Versatile cordyline makes a wonderful contribution to the tropical-style garden. Offering handsome foliage shapes as well as brilliant leaf colours, it is undemanding and easy to grow. The satiny leaves are arranged around an upright stem that can grow to 3 metres (10 ft) high, branching with maturity. A wide range of impressive cultivars—of varying heights and leaf shapes—has been developed. And the colour range is amazing: crimson, bronze or green leaves, striped or edged with pink, cream, yellow or with rainbow combinations. There are many dwarf and compact varieties. These forms make a colourful understorey to palms, either massed or as accent plants. Tis are also excellent container plants for terraces and balconies.

GROWING NOTES
Suitable for warm, subtropical and tropical climates, most tis do not tolerate frost but can cope with salt winds. They are best grown in partial shade to prevent scorching from the sun. Any soil will do, provided it drains freely, although they benefit from regular fertilizing to speed growth and intensify leaf colour. Apply a thick layer of mulch to conserve moisture.

Vibrant, exotic and versatile, *Cordyline fruticosa* cultivars bring colour and character to the garden and make a bold statement indoors.

NEVER-NEVER PLANT

Outdoors in warm climates or indoors in a pot, the colours of the never-never plant can be as bold as bright green and gold or as subtle as silvery green.

Awkward by name but handsome by nature, ctenanthe (the 'c' is silent) provides interesting contrast to the more showy foliage plants. *C. oppenheimiana* features slender, oblong leaves with a herringbone pattern of green and silver teamed with reddish undersides. It grows to about 60 cm (2 ft) high and curiously hangs its leaves upside down on a cold night. *C. lubbersiana* is a little taller and features irregular bands of green and gold. The never-never plant spreads from a light rhizome and can be used as a massed groundcover or understorey plant in suitable climates. Elsewhere, it is an easy-care indoor plant appreciated for the subtle beauty of its leaves.

GROWING NOTES

This Brazilian native enjoys a warm and humid climate with a minimum temperature of about 13°C (55°F). It needs a lightly shaded position—if it has too much shade, it will lose the intensity of its leaf colour. The never-never plant requires ample water during the summer months and shelter from strong winds. Indoors, place the plant in a brightly lit position and mist regularly to increase the humidity.

ENSETE VENTRICOSUM
ABYSSINIAN BANANA

It looks like an edible banana, but the Abyssinian banana is in a different genus and is a far more spectacular plant. The lush bright green leaves, up to 3.5 metres (12 ft) long, have a prominent, rhubarb-red midvein. They form a dense crown above a single, trunk-like false stem. Its pendulous flower spikes, up to 3 metres (10 ft) long, have white flowers within red-bronze bracts. The Abyssinian banana grows to 6 metres (20 ft) tall. Although the banana-like fruits are not edible, the seeds and the flower heads are cooked and eaten in its native Africa. After flowering, individual plants die and are cut to the ground. Use this unusual plant as a feature or accent.

Fast growing and very lush, the Abyssinian banana has flamboyant foliage that instantly evokes a wonderful tropical ambience.

GROWING NOTES
Abyssinian banana does not tolerate frost and is best grown in a tropical or subtropical climate. It prefers full sun or part shade, with shelter from strong winds. Enrich a well-drained soil with organic matter and provide ample water in summer.

FARFUGIUM JAPONICUM (SYN. *LIGULARIA TUSSILAGINEA*)
LEOPARD PLANT

The leopard plant is a handy specimen to have in any garden. The reason? This handsome perennial can provide foliage colour in shady positions in cool climates. The bright gold spots that liberally spatter its glossy green leaves literally light up dark areas with their glow. Leopard plants are particularly effective when mass-planted to maximize their impact, but they also do well in pots. Growing to 40–60 cm (16–24 inches) high, the large circular leaves are held almost horizontally on long stems to best display the vivid patterns. Of several cultivars, 'Aureomaculatum' is most commonly grown. The flowers are small, yellow daisies in a loose cluster but are not particularly pretty.

GROWING NOTES

Native to Japan, the leopard plant is frost hardy to about −5°C (23°F) and prefers cool, moist climates. It will grow in warm regions but is unsuitable for the tropics. It prefers dappled sunlight or partial shade, with shelter from strong winds. This plant prefers a fertile, moist soil with a mulch of compost to prevent the roots from drying out.

The gold-speckled leaves of the hardy leopard plant can brighten up a dark corner of the garden, providing vibrant, contrasting foliage for cool-climate gardens.

GUZMANIA SPECIES AND CULTIVARS
GUZMANIA

Guzmanias are part of the fascinating bromeliad family. They grow on branches, in forks of trees or in leaf litter on the forest floor. There are hundreds of species and cultivars, bred for spectacular foliage colour as well as their showy flowers. They form a perfect rosette shape, with satiny leaves that have no spines. Although many have rich green leaves, foliage colours include shades of pink, red, orange, yellow and cream and may be striped or banded. The central leaves may become brightly coloured at flowering time. Their glorious flower spikes are red, yellow and orange, and last for months.

Guzmanias are ideal houseplants, offering dramatic form, striking coloured foliage and beautiful, long-lasting flowers—all in one low-maintenance package.

GROWING NOTES

Outside the tropics and subtropics, guzmanias are best grown indoors. They are sensitive to cold and wet winters, but should be misted regularly in summer to increase humidity. Use a coarse orchid mix to provide the necessary open drainage. Choose a brightly lit position, sheltered from direct sun and wind, and keep the central vase filled with water.

HELICONIA SPECIES
LOBSTER CLAW, PARROT FLOWER

Few flowers can be as wildly improbable and utterly spectacular as the lobster claw. Beloved by florists for their size, dramatic form and long-lasting qualities, the display actually comes from colourful, pointed bracts, which enclose the insignificant true flowers. Some species such as *H. rostrata* and *H. stricta* carry the blooms in long, pendulous strings of spectacular construction. They have huge, banana-like leaves and grow into large clumps. *H. psittacorum*, the parrot flower, has smaller blooms of yellow, orange or red held aloft slender upright stems, and is ideal for mass-planting. It grows to around 1–1.5 metres (3–5 ft) in height.

GROWING NOTES

Lobster claws are related to bananas and bird of paradise, but are more sensitive to cold than these plants. They demand high humidity and temperatures above 15°C (60°F) to flower reliably. The soil should be rich in organic matter, well drained and in a position that has filtered, bright light. In colder areas helconias require a heated conservatory or glasshouse, as they die down in response to the cold.

Lobster claws may be available to most of us only as exotic cut flowers, but if you live in the tropics they flower in the garden for most of the year.

HIBISCUS ROSA-SINENSIS CULTIVARS
CHINESE HIBISCUS, HAWAIIAN HIBISCUS

Hibiscus are fast growing and long living, and provide the classic tropical-resort look to gardens in warm areas.

From humble origins in southern China, cultivars of this popular hibiscus are now synonymous with South Pacific holiday destinations such as Hawaii, Fiji and Malaysia. They are evergreen, bushy shrubs of 2–4 metres (6–12 ft) in height, with handsome foliage and very characteristic, open, bell-shaped flowers. Individual blooms last for only a day or two, but are borne in profusion from late spring to winter. The flowers come in every imaginable shade of red, yellow, orange, pink and white, with bicolours and subtle shadings in many combinations. Blooming varieties can include single, semi-double and double, with individual flowers up to 26 cm (10 inches) in width. Use for informal hedges, or as screening or foundation shrubs to create a tropical look. They're also an excellent choice to grow near a swimming pool.

GROWING NOTES

Hibiscus need a frost-free climate and a sunny position, and they enjoy humidity. As heavy feeders, they thrive in a rich soil with regular applications of organic matter and water. Prune them up to one half of their bulk in early spring.

HOSTA SPECIES AND CULTIVARS
PLANTAIN LILIES

The foliage patterns offered by plantain lilies are always understated, never gaudy, and centre around green, blue, cream and gold. The delicate flowers are usually mauve.

In cool climates, plantain lilies are an essential component of the lush foliage garden. Their decorative leaves vary in size, colour, texture and pattern. Hundreds of cultivars have been bred, from dwarf forms at less than 10 cm (4 inches) high to statuesque clumps over 90 cm (3 ft) tall. Leaf colours range from steely blue to chartreuse with every shade of green in between. Many have beautiful variegations in white, cream or yellow. In some forms, the leaf surface is shiny; in others, they're matt or powdery, or perhaps puckered or corrugated. Plantain lilies form dense, circular clumps that are ideal for mass-planting in woodland areas or near ponds and water features. Variegated and bright lime forms bring light into shady areas and can be used to highlight garden ornaments. To add to their charms, hostas also bear pretty flowers from early summer. The bell-shaped blooms are held above the foliage on long stems; they are usually mauve but can be white or purple. Some, such as *H. plantaginea* and its cultivars, are fragrant.

Plantain lilies die down in winter to survive the cold. In late spring the fleshy underground rhizome sends up firm shoots

that rapidly develop into dome-shaped mounds of lush foliage. As a general rule, the gold and gold-variegated cultivars will take more sun than the others and the white variegated types need the most shade. Blue-leaved cultivars will lose their colour if grown in too much shade.

GROWING NOTES

Plantain lilies are suitable for cool to mild areas, but a few species will tolerate warm climates. They like slightly acidic, very rich soils that hold moisture but still drain well. To improve growth and vigour, dig in copious amounts of compost, leaf mould and other organic materials. The other secrets to success are heavy mulching each spring and autumn and a balanced fertilizer in spring and summer. Plantain lilies particularly need even and generous watering to keep their lush, open leaves in prime condition. Snails and slugs will love these plants even more than you, so control is necessary.

Plantain lilies are outstanding foliage plants for cool, shady gardens. The simple elegance of their leaves has a sculptural quality that works well in mass-plantings.

MANDEVILLA SPECIES AND CULTIVARS
CHILEAN JASMINE

Chilean jasmine is one of the loveliest climbers, bearing profuse clusters of trumpet-shaped flowers over a long period. All species climb by gentle twining, and are generally fast growing without becoming rampant. *Mandevilla laxa* delights with large white flowers that have a heady fragrance. 'Alice du Pont', a cultivar of *M.* x *amabilis*, has particularly large, deep-pink blooms. *M. sanderi* (syn. *Dipladenia sanderi*) has glossy leaves and flowers of soft rose-pink with a bright-yellow throat. This species and its cultivars 'Red Riding Hood' (bright pink), 'My Fair Lady' (pale pink) and 'Scarlet Pimpernel' (crimson) are wonderful in pots to climb pillars or pruned to form softly tumbling shrubs.

The pretty Chilean jasmine needs only a light support to twine across walls and fences or around columns and posts. In warm areas it flowers for most of the year.

GROWING NOTES

Generally, Chilean jasmine needs a frost-free climate. 'Alice du Pont' is the least tolerant to cold while *M. laxa* may withstand light frosts and is deciduous in cool areas. In cold climates, Chilean jasmine thrives in greenhouses and conservatories. They like a well-drained, enriched soil, sun to partial shade and regular water, especially during the summer months.

PASSIFLORA SPECIES
PASSIONFRUIT, PASSION FLOWER

The flavour and aroma of its fruit are well known, but the versatile passionfruit can be used for screening, decorating a fence or providing shade over a pergola. *Passiflora edulis* is just one of 400 species of evergreen, tendril climbers that have lush foliage, fabulous flowers and often tasty fruit. The flowers are intricately formed, with starry petals and prominent stamens, often in white, mauve and purple combinations. The brilliant red flowers of *P. coccinea* are especially large but its fruit is not as delicious. All passionfruit species are very fast, vigorous growers; with the aid of netting or wire they will rapidly cover a fence, pergola or shed with their dense and lush foliage.

GROWING NOTES

Originating in tropical South America, *P. edulis* and *P. coccinea* need a warm, frost-free climate and rich, well-drained soil. These plants are heavy feeders so will respond well to regular applications of fertilizer and water, plus an organic mulch around the roots. Prune plants to contain their growth in late winter before flowering commences in spring. They need full sun as well as protection from wind.

Edible passionfruit are ripe when they turn purple and start to wrinkle, but they are worth growing for their exotic blossoms. The red-flowering passionfruit is spectacular in full bloom.

PHILODENDRON BIPINNATIFIDUM SYN. P. SELLOUM
TREE PHILODENDRON

With its mass of large, lush, green leaves *Philodendron bipinnatifidum* makes a splendid accent for a tropical garden.

Philodendrons include many well-known houseplants, but *P. bipinnatifidum* is the big daddy of them all. Its glossy, deeply lobed leaves can be up to 1 metre (3 ft) long, on sturdy leaf stalks of the same length. They grow in a rosette shape and, over time, develop a woody stem, supported by long aerial roots. In tropical gardens, this plant can climb high into trees, covering the tree trunk in a cloak of lush green. It is ideal for filling a corner, or binding large shady banks where other plants might struggle. Dwarf cultivars such as 'Xanadu' are only about 40 cm (16 inches) tall and can be densely massed as a groundcover. Indoors, philodendrons are almost indestructible, withstanding low light, draughts and airconditioning, but they need plenty of room to spread.

GROWING NOTES

Native to Brazil, the philodendron needs a warm to tropical climate to grow outdoors. Although tough enough to survive full sun and poor soils, it looks and performs best in light shade with a rich, well-drained soil.

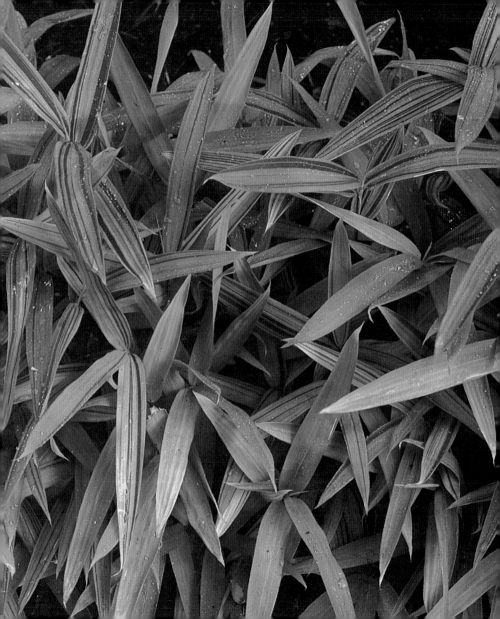

PLEIOBLASTUS SPECIES
DWARF BAMBOO

The dwarf bamboo has a lot going for it—dense and vigorous growth, evergreen foliage and it grows well in cool climates. It also comes in striped variegations, making it an ideal ornamental plant. These include *P. viridistriatus* with its golden-yellow new growth, ageing to striped leaves and *P. variegatus*, which features variable white striping and grows to around 75 cm (30 inches). Both species will retain their colouring in low light. The true dwarf bamboo, *P. pygmaeus*, reaches only 30–40 cm (12–16 inches) with bright green foliage. These bamboos are running types that spread indefinitely unless controlled with root barriers or grown in containers. They can be useful to control erosion as the spreading rhizomes make an excellent soil binder.

Use dwarf bamboo as a neat, evergreen edging by installing a root barrier to check its spread. Its texture is particularly appealing.

GROWING NOTES

All dwarf bamboos are frost hardy and suit cool to warm areas. They grow easily, preferring a loose, well-drained soil enriched with organic matter and ample water. Cut them back in late winter to promote new growth and to contain their size.

PLUMERIA SPECIES AND CULTIVARS
FRANGIPANI

It's impossible to pass by a frangipani tree in full bloom without plucking a flower from the tree or rescuing one of dozens carpeting the ground, to tuck behind your ear.

A frangipani tree in bloom is one of life's great pleasures. Its waxy blooms have an endearing simplicity and a sweet, fresh fragrance that is uplifting rather than cloying. Colours range from white, blushing to sunny yellow centres, to perhaps deep crimson or any shade of a tropical sunrise. The gorgeous shades of pink, apricot and peach, usually flushing more golden towards the centre, are a sight to behold.

Most frangipanis are deciduous trees, growing to 6–8 metres (18–24 ft) high and almost as wide in a broadly domed shape. The bare branches are thick and fleshy with a wonderfully regular branching pattern. One species, *P. obtusa*, is evergreen in tropical climates and flowers for much of the year. *P. rubra* also loves the heat, and its form, *acutifolia*, is the most widely grown in gardens. It has long, pointed leaves and offers a wide choice of flower colours, borne in profusion during summer.

Frangipanis are superb feature trees, often grown against the warmest wall of the house where heat is reflected and absorbed. They will grow in pots if kept fairly dry. The flowers are used extensively in decoration—floating in small water bowls, or threaded together to form floral necklaces and wreaths that are used to adorn religious icons. Grow from stem cuttings or large branches taken in winter. Leave cuttings to dry out for a few weeks before planting. The milky white sap of the frangipani tree can irritate the skin and is poisonous.

GROWING NOTES
Originally from Central America, frangipanis thrive in the tropics and subtropics but can be grown in cooler conditions if they have protection from frost. They thrive in full sun and prefer a rich, well-drained soil but are not particularly fussy.

Frangipani flowers are loved for their beauty and fresh fragrance. Set against a background of lush, mid-green leaves in the form of a dense canopy, they are a visual delight.

The handsome pickerel weed looks best in large clumps, either planted directly into the soil at the pond edge or in a pot.

PONTEDERIA CORDATA
PICKEREL WEED

Pickerel weed is an aquatic plant that's grown for its handsome foliage and dense spikes of usually blue flowers. Indigenous to both North and South America, this perennial grows in a clump to about 1 metre (3 ft) high. Its stems are rounded and spongy and leaves can be heart- or arrow-shaped. Although pickerel weed grows from a creeping rhizome, it does not become invasive as do many water-loving plants. The densely packed spikes of intense-blue flowers are borne from summer to autumn, after most other marginal plants have finished flowering. A white form is also available.

GROWING NOTES

The robust pickerel weed thrives in most climates, from tropical to very cold. It grows in water up to 30 cm (12 inches) deep, but tolerates shallow pools or boggy ground, where it will grow rather shorter and stockier. Flowering is best in full sun.

SETARIA PALMIFOLIA
PALM GRASS

One of the finest ornamental grasses, palm grass provides a wonderful rippling texture with its rich green foliage. The bold, arching leaves are beautifully pleated and resemble the foliage of young palms. In frost-free climates clumps can reach to 2.4 metres (8 ft) tall; in temperate climates or drier locations, they are much shorter. Foxtail-like flower spikes are produced in summer and soar above the foliage. In tropical and subtropical areas where palm grass sets seed freely, flower heads must be removed to avoid weed problems. In drier and colder locations it does not appear to set seed. Palm grass is effective when mass-planted to maximize its textural impact, or it can be used as a background for exotic flowers or as a stunning specimen in a large container.

GROWING NOTES
Palm grass tolerates very moist soils such as bordering ponds but is also drought tolerant once established. It grows in full sun to part shade in any soil type. It struggles in temperatures below 5°C (40°F) and will die back over winter in cold areas.

Although a true grass, palm grass imparts an exotic tropical ambience. Its height varies greatly, according to climate.

SOLANDRA MAXIMA
CUP OF GOLD

Big, bold and rampant, cup of gold is a magnificent climber that thrives in tropical to subtropical gardens. The creamy yellow blooms are huge, up to 25 cm (10 inches) wide and the rate of growth is astonishing in favourable conditions. Cup of gold needs room to spread and a sturdy support, so it's a good idea to tie and train the woody vine early in the piece. Flowering is over a long period, from spring to autumn, and each bloom has a distinctive purplish stripe down the centre of each petal. Use cup of gold in large gardens and in coastal areas as it withstands strong sea winds.

GROWING NOTES

Dramatic, chalice-shaped flowers are the star attraction of this robust, large-growing climber. An unusual variegated form is much less vigorous.

A native of tropical Mexico, cup of gold needs a frost-free climate but it is fairly forgiving about soil type as long as drainage is good. Best results are in soils that are enriched with organic matter and are regularly watered in summer. Grow in full sun for maximum flowering. It can be pruned after flowering or whenever necessary to contain its spread.

SOLENOSTEMON SCUTELLARIOIDES
COLEUS

For brilliant colour, and lots of it, dynamic coleus fits the bill perfectly. In very warm climates it is a short-lived perennial but in more temperate areas it is grown as an annual. Its soft leaves are as highly coloured and patterned as its flowers, featuring myriad variations of red, pink, green, yellow, bronze and cream. Some varieties have simple leaves with serrated edges, others are deeply lobed and dissected. In comparison, the flowers are unremarkable, being pale blue on a small spike (and can be removed where leaf colour only is desired). Use coleus for splashes of bright colour in the garden. It also makes a great border or bedding plant, and can be grown in pots indoors in a well-lit position.

Coleus grows rapidly to about 60 cm (24 inches) high and offers a blaze of colour and interesting patterns. Remove the flowers to help prolong the life of the plant.

GROWING NOTES

In warm areas coleus enjoys a sheltered position with light shade. The leaves are very sensitive to frost and hot sun. A rich soil and ample watering in summer give best results. Pinch out the tips to promote bushiness and use the tips for cuttings.

TRADESCANTIA SPECIES AND HYBRIDS
SPIDERWORT

There are some pretty flowering perennials and coloured-foliage groundcovers bearing the name spiderwort. The Andersoniana Group (syn. *T. virginiana*) includes hybrids with delicate, three-petalled flowers that come in lovely hues of pink, mauve, purple, violet or white. Set against a background of grass-like leaves in clumps that grow to 60 cm (2 ft) tall, the flowers open in the morning and close by midday, but there is a constant succession. Use these herbaceous perennials in beds and borders or as an understorey plant in lush foliage gardens.

T. zebrina or silver inch plant, has sparkling foliage, banded in silver and purplish green with pink flowers. It forms a low, dense groundcover that is ideal for highlighting around the base of taller feature plants or garden ornaments, or trailing from a hanging basket.

GROWING NOTES

Andersoniana spiderworts grow in a range of climates. Cut them near the ground in midsummer to promote a second flowering. *T. zebrina* is frost sensitive, but all *Tradescantia* species enjoy partial shade and moist, even damp, rich soil.

Top and opposite: The Andersoniana spiderworts are valued for their pretty and dainty spring flowers. Above: *T. zebrina* has striped, silver-green leaves with purple undersides.

ZANTEDESCHIA AETHIOPICA
ARUM LILY

The stately, elegant blooms of arum lilies are well known as cut flowers, but the whole plant can contribute valuable foliage texture to the garden. Arum lilies love wet feet, making them especially useful in damp spots that other plants reject. Mass them in, or at the edge of, shallow ponds and watch them thrive. Keep them in check as in some warm areas they have become an invasive weed in waterways. The species grows to more than 1 metre (3 ft) in height but there are smaller hybrids available such as 'Childsiana'. Although the flowers are mostly pure white, the cultivar, 'Green Goddess', features green markings on the flowers. A blushing-pink form is sold as 'Marshmallow' or 'Pink Mist'.

The elegant blooms of the arum lily flower from spring to autumn on long stems among lush, clumping foliage.

GROWING NOTES

Arum lilies need protection from frost and hot sun. They prefer a rich soil that is constantly moist or wet. In warm climates, they are easy to grow and stay evergreen if given sufficient water. As the broad, arrowhead leaves and thick stems are very soft, they need shelter from the wind.

palms

Whether fringing a coral island, accenting a rainforest or greening a desert oasis, palms are some of the most evocative plants on the planet. While their size and shape may vary, they have in common those classic, lush, green divided fronds.

Palms are easy to grow, requiring little maintenance. In the garden, pots or conservatory, palms create interest and a wonderful ambience.

Palms grow as a single, unbranched trunk with a crown of leaves at the top. They have only one growing point at the centre where all the new leaves emerge, and if this point is destroyed the whole plant dies. Some palms have a clumping habit, but these are simply multiples of the same unbranched stems. They have fibrous root systems with all roots developing from the same point at the base of the trunk, forming a compact and dense rootball. This is one of the reasons they grow so well in pots and makes them ideal landscaping plants in small areas.

There are more than 2500 species of palms, most of which come from subtropical and tropical climates, but a few grow in cooler areas. Palms are important commercially and are the source of products such as dates, coconuts, palm oil, palm sugar and coconut fibre or coir. In local communities the trunks are used for timber and the leaves for thatching.

Palms vary in height from 1.5 metres (5 ft) to a whopping 27 metres (90 ft) or more. With such variety in size as well as form, palms can be grown in most climates, both indoors and out. They are versatile, too—use them to form a stately avenue for a driveway, mix them with lush foliage plants to create a tropical ambience or simply grow them in pots. If opting for a lush, tropical effect, palms look their best when planted in

Clockwise from top left: The windmill palm (*Trachycarpus fortunei*); the red stems of lipstick palm (*Cyrtostachys renda*) and circular leaves of *Licuala*; dracaenas combine well with palms; and tall cabbage tree palms (*Livistona australis*). Previous page: Graceful palm fronds are instantly recognizable, but despite their delicate appearance, most are easy to grow.

Palms are ideal for poolside plantings as they are tidy and low maintenance. They also add a special ambience to the area. Combine plants of various heights for the best effect.

Opposite: The parlour palm, *Chamaedorea elegans*, is one of the smallest palms. With its pretty foliage and tolerance of deep shade, it is a favourite indoor plant.

groups. Use palms of varying heights mixed with plants with contrasting foliage textures to avoid creating an area with lots of tall bare trunks. The clumping types can make effective screens as they become thicker, rather than taller, as they grow. Palms are both tidy and low-maintenance plants, making them ideal to grow around swimming pools. But avoid those species that have sharp spines for safety reasons. All but the largest palms make excellent pot plants, either outdoors on terraces, patios, balconies and in courtyards, or indoors as houseplants or conservatory specimens.

COLD TOLERANCE

Some palms will stray outside their subtropical home, tolerating lower temperatures and even light frosts. The most cold tolerant is probably the windmill palm, *Trachycarpus fortunei*, which has a rounded crown of fan-shaped fronds and grows to around 12 metres (40 ft). It can tolerate temperatures to −15°C (5°F) when mature, and is unsuitable for the tropics. The Mediterranean fan palm, *Chamaerops humilis*, grows to about 5 metres (15 ft) in poor soil and dry climates, withstanding temperatures to −10°C (14°F) for short periods. Both *Livistona chinensis*, Chinese fan palm, and *Phoenix canariensis*, Canary Island date palm, can tolerate temperatures

to −5°C (23°F) for short periods. Chinese fan palm has a large crown of broad, cascading fronds and usually grows to around 5 metres (15 ft) in gardens. The majestic Canary Island date palm grows to 20 metres (60 ft) and is very salt tolerant. The clumping palm, *Rhapis excelsa* (lady palm) is frost tolerant and grows in a wide range of climates. Other palms that withstand light frosts include *Washingtonia filifera*, the desert fan palm, which reaches 15 metres (50 ft) and the jelly palm, *Butia capitata*. This lovely palm features silvery fronds and edible fruits; it can grow to 6 metres (20 ft) tall.

CLUMPING PALMS

Where screening and lush foliage effects are required rather than height, the clumping palms come into their own. The bamboo palm, *Chamaedorea seifrizii*, is most effective, forming clumps of slender stems. It grows well in warm temperate climates to around 3 metres (10 ft) tall. Golden cane palm, *Dypsis lutescens*, makes a dense and dramatic clump of gold-tinged stems with a graceful arching habit. It can reach 10 metres (30 ft) in the tropics but is much smaller in gardens. One of the most beautiful—and tough—clumping palms is *Rhapis excelsa*, the lady palm. This slow-growing beauty forms a dense mass of stems with glossy, fan-shaped leaves that are

Clockwise from top left: Blend some palms, tree ferns and cordylines for a lush look; cabbage tree palm; golden cane palm; and fan palm.

divided into finger-like segments. The clump can reach 5 metres (15 ft) in height but it is usually around 2.5 metres (8 ft). Clumping palms are also reliable indoor plants.

GROWING NOTES

Palms differ in the amount of sun and shade they require. A partially shaded position or dappled light is ideal for most, but some species, including *Butia*, *Washingtonia*, *Trachycarpus* and *Chamaerops*, prefer full sun. Young palms tend to need protection and become more sun tolerant as they get older. Too much shade causes palms with silver leaves or golden stems to lose their colour. Most palms require good drainage and thrive in soils that are enriched with organic matter such as compost, leaf mould and manures. For best results, water regularly in summer and apply complete fertilizer in spring.

Most palms do not require pruning other than removal of old fronds, and some are 'self-cleaning' and do it themselves. Indoor plants will benefit from regular misting to increase humidity and an application of liquid fertilizer each spring.

Palms with a clumping habit make good screening plants and mix beautifully with the finely divided fronds of tree ferns. The bamboo palm (*Chamaedorea seifrizii*) and the lady palm (*Rhapis excelsa*) are excellent examples.

A long, narrow, ribbon-like leaf that curves or droops is known as a strap. And these 'strappies' provide the exuberant foliage that sprouts from clumping plants, giving them their wonderful forms and shapes. Curvaceous and soft in appearance, strappies contrast beautifully with sharp, angular or spreading plants. They're useful plants too—for borders, edging,

Strappies, like these clivias, add height, texture and volume to a garden and contrast with the straight edge of a path. Previous pages: Use strappy plants, such as water iris, as a vertical accent plant around a water feature.

underplantings, features and potted plants. Strappies also exhibit gorgeous colours, rich textures and interesting forms. The evergreens provide lush green foliage and smooth textures all year round. Others produce brilliant seasonal colour in the form of bands, spots, stripes, splashes and everything in between. And the best part is, there are strappies to suit all climates.

Daylilies are among the most generous of flowering strappies with a succession of summer blooms.
Following pages: Use strappies in clumps for bold accents amid rounded shrubs and cushions of trailing plants.

AGAPANTHUS PRAECOX SUBSPECIES *ORIENTALIS*
AGAPANTHUS, NILE LILY

A line of agapanthus adds a formal element to a warm-climate garden. For a beautiful, long-lasting summer display, plant a mix of classic lilac-blue and white forms.

Agapanthus epitomizes the strappy plant. Its ribbon-like evergreen leaves form a rounded clump that grows from 15 cm (6 inches) to more than 1 metre (3 ft) high as well as wide. This versatile plant looks spectacular as an edging for a wall, driveway or pathway, massed as a groundcover or simply grown in a pot. In late spring and summer, stiff stems topped by a ball of lily-like blue, white or mauve flowers appear from the leafy clumps. Agapanthus is quick to establish and easy to divide. Its strong, fleshy root systems can bind soil.

GROWING NOTES

Agapanthus enjoys a warm, frost-free climate and relishes life in full sun and moist, well-drained soil. If planted in the shade it won't produce as many flowers as it would in the sun but it will have lots of strappy leaves. In cold and frost-prone areas, plant either deciduous forms that are dormant over winter or evergreen perennials in pots in a protected spot. After flowering, cut the stems to the ground to remove seed heads and tidy the clumps. Divide the clumps in spring.

BULBINELLA FLORIBUNDA
CAT'S TAIL

For dynamic spring colour, the exceptionally showy cat's tail is hard to beat. Its torch-like golden flowers sit on tall straight stems that stand above the 60 cm- (2 ft-) high strappy, somewhat untidy leaves. In the garden, the flowers will last a month or more as the blooms gradually open along the spires. Their golden yellow colour provides a striking contrast to the blues and purples of early-spring pansies, anemones, star flowers (*Ipheion uniflorum*) and aquilegias. Cat's tail makes an excellent, long-lasting cut flower.

Cat's tails' vibrant, golden-yellow display lasts for several weeks, starting in late winter or early spring.

GROWING NOTES

Although classified as a bulb, cat's tail grows from a fibrous root system rather than from a bulb. It is an ideal choice for a Mediterranean garden as it is dormant in summer. A South African native, cat's tail thrives in most cool to temperate gardens in sun or partial shade, as long as it doesn't dry out. The plants are slightly frost tender so they will need protection in cold climates. Established clumps can be divided in autumn before regrowth begins. Plant new clumps so the crown is at soil level. Do not allow the roots to dry out.

CLIVIA MINIATA
CLIVIA, KAFFIR LILY

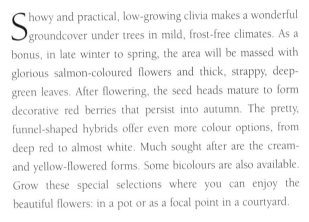

Clivias enjoy the dry shade and shelter of trees and palms. Their leaves make a lush, green groundcover all year round and there are beautiful blooms in late winter and spring.

Showy and practical, low-growing clivia makes a wonderful groundcover under trees in mild, frost-free climates. As a bonus, in late winter to spring, the area will be massed with glorious salmon-coloured flowers and thick, strappy, deep-green leaves. After flowering, the seed heads mature to form decorative red berries that persist into autumn. The pretty, funnel-shaped hybrids offer even more colour options, from deep red to almost white. Much sought after are the cream- and yellow-flowered forms. Some bicolours are also available. Grow these special selections where you can enjoy the beautiful flowers: in a pot or as a focal point in a courtyard.

GROWING NOTES

Clivias grow from offshoots, by dividing a mature clump or from seed. They tolerate a dry, shaded position (which is why they thrive under trees) but benefit from extra water in dry times. They need to be protected from cold and frost. In cold-winter areas, grow clivias as indoor or conservatory plants.

CROCOSMIA X CROCOSMIIFLORA
CROCOSMIA, MONTBRETIA

The fiery orange flowers of crocosmia erupt like fireworks out of the strappy, green foliage, providing seasonal interest amid lush greenery.

Crocosmias are the pyrotechnic wonders of the garden world, full of vibrant, explosive colour. In late spring and summer, orange or yellow spires of flowers erupt from clumps of bright green leaves. Once summer flowering has finished, the plants die back. Crocosmias are the perfect plants to bring excitement to a massed garden bed. Allow them to form large clumps for maximum impact. They'll add a shot of colour to a blue-and-white garden or give an energetic jolt to an all-green scheme. Create a bright fiery display by combining crocosmia with other orange, yellow and red plants such as marigolds and dahlias. For large, colourful flowers, select any of the named varieties such as 'Lucifer' or 'Bressingham Blaze'.

GROWING NOTES

Crocosmias grow in sun or shade in well-drained soil. Plant corms in autumn or winter. In some areas they may become weedy, but their lack of pests and diseases and their bold flowers make them welcome plants in most gardens. Divide overcrowded clumps in spring or after flowering as the foliage dies. Water well through summer.

CYMBOPOGON CITRATUS
LEMON GRASS

With lemon grass, you can have your clump and eat it too. Lemon grass can be used as a feature plant in a herb garden or grown as a striking accent among shrubs or perennials. It will even grow as a potted plant in a sunny courtyard. Lemon grass has coarse, ribbon-like leaves and forms a grassy clump. It will grow quickly to form a large, imposing mass 1–1.5 metres (3–4 ft) tall. As its name suggests, the leaves have a lemony aroma. Its stems are harvested for cooking and its leaves make an aromatic tea.

GROWING NOTES

Lemon grass likes full sun and excellent drainage. Start off new plants in spring. Before planting, dig well-rotted manure or compost into the soil. Give the plants plenty of water to promote growth and start harvesting stems in summer. Liquid-feed once a month from spring to early autumn for good growth. In cold areas, lemon grass needs a warm spot to protect it from frost. Divide the clumps in early spring.

Large clumps of lemon grass give dramatic impact in a herb garden, pot or among flowers. The shoots of lemon grass are widely used as a flavouring in Asian cuisine, particularly Thai cooking. The leaves of this versatile plant can be brewed to make a refreshing tea.

EUCOMIS SPECIES
PINEAPPLE LILY

The crowning tufts of leaves at the tip of the flower stalk give *Eucomis* its common name. This striking plant creates interest when mass-planted or as a feature.

The flowers of the pineapple lily must be seen to be believed. Tiny star-shaped cream or pink flowers are tightly packed into each stem and each stalk is topped with a pineapple-like tuft. Equally impressive are the rosettes of wave-shaped, glossy green leaves. Some species, such as *E. comosa*, have stems and leaves with purple spots. To make the most of the handsome foliage, mass plants together in a garden bed or use as a tall groundcover to 30–60 cm (1–2 ft) tall. Most species flower in summer and autumn.

GROWING NOTES

The pineapple lily likes sun to partial shade and a warm, frost-free spot. In cold areas, grow them in pots and in winter, they'll need to go indoors. Flowers appear in summer and may curve over with the weight of the blooms. If the stems remain upright, leave the stems until flowering has finished as the seed heads are most attractive. Plants die back in autumn and are dormant over winter, which is the time to divide clumps. The pineapple lily grows easily from seed.

GLADIOLUS SPECIES
GLADIOLUS

The tall, large-flowered gladiolus is a well-known display plant widely grown for use as a cut flower. It falls in and out of fashion, particularly in flower arrangements. Its distinguishing features include funnel-shaped blooms and sword-like leaves on long rigid stems. And it comes in a wide range of gorgeous colours. For a softer, less dramatic effect, species gladiolus, with their dainty clumps, will fit the bill. Reliable forms include painted lady, *G. carneus* (white, pink or mauve flowers blotched with purple or yellow), and the miniature *G.* x *colvillei*, best known as 'The Bride', which has white flowers and only grows to around 40 cm (16 inches) tall.

GROWING NOTES

Gladiolus is grown from a corm. In warm climates, plant corms in autumn, but in colder climates, wait until spring. Plants need little extra care other than regular watering and grooming to remove spent flowers and discoloured leaves. Species gladiolus likes a sunny spot and well-drained soil. Most gladioli die back in autumn and winter after flowering. In cold areas, lift corms and store over winter in a warm, dry spot.

Bold and dramatic or soft and elegant, the choice is yours with the versatile gladiolus. For a stiff cut flower, select a tall hybrid and pick as the flowers begin to open. The dainty *Gladiolus* x *colvillei* 'The Bride' (opposite) offers a softer look with masses of pretty white blooms.

HEMEROCALLIS SPECIES
DAYLILY

Bright and cheerful daylilies provide wonderful contrasting colour in a mixed garden bed in summer. The flowers last only a day, but the profusion of buds means plenty of blooms for several months.

The beautiful daylily is an ideal perennial to grow in warm-climate gardens. Grown in a leafy clump, it produces spectacular stems of flowers in a range of dazzling colours. Individual flowers last only for a day, but as the plants produce many stems, daylilies will bloom for several months, from spring into autumn. Place daylilies in clumps in a flower garden, using their bold colour as an accent or their soft shape to contrast with upright, rigid plants. These plants look stunning when grown along a cottage-garden fence or use a miniature variety as a feature in a pot. All parts of the daylily are edible.

GROWING NOTES

Plant daylilies in a sunny spot in well-drained soil that doesn't dry out. Dig in lots of well-rotted organic material. Evergreen daylilies grow well in warm gardens while deciduous species are better suited to cold and frosty areas. Remove spent stems to make way for more flowers. Divide clumps every three years in autumn or in spring in cold climates. Daylilies give brighter colour when grown in partial shade.

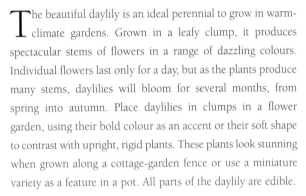

IRIS SPECIES
WATER IRIS

R enowned for its striking beauty, the long-flowering iris will enhance any garden. Particularly attractive is the water-loving flag iris, such as *I. pseudacorus*, which has graceful leaves to 1 metre (3 ft) high and tall stems of yellow flowers. A clump makes a dramatic statement next to a pond or any moist area. For extra interest, look for variegated forms that bring foliage colour, especially in spring. Also happy beside or in water is the Japanese iris, *I. ensata* (syn. *I. kaempferi*), with its large flowers in shades of white, blue, lavender or purple. In cool climates, *I. sibirica* forms bold vertical clumps around 60–120 cm (2–4 ft) high. It produces attractive blue, mauve or white flowers from spring into summer.

GROWING NOTES

Irises grow in a range of conditions, from hot and dry to literally in water, so it is vital to match the species with the correct growing conditions. All like sun, but most of the water-loving species mentioned here need shade in hot climates. Grow iris by dividing established clumps after flowering. Prune to remove spent flower stems and discoloured leaves.

In tropical and warm areas, choose a water-loving iris, like the multicoloured Japanese form, *I. ensata* (above) or the sunny yellow *I. pseudacorus* (opposite).

LIRIOPE MUSCARI
LIRIOPE, RIBBON GRASS

Lovely liriope is a useful ornamental grass that grows well in most climates. It is one of the few plants that will grow happily in sun or shade so it is an ideal choice as a ribbon border for unifying a garden. Plants range in height from a tiny 20 cm (8 inches) up to 60 cm (2 ft) for the giant forms. Particularly striking are the white-and-green-striped varieties, such as *L. muscari* 'Variegata'. The spires of lily flowers, in shades of mauve, purple or white, make a bold contrast to the green or variegated leaves. Liriope also makes an effective groundcover. The dwarf varieties perform beautifully too, especially as edging for a pathway.

A simple planting of liriope alongside a pathway or used as a border adds interesting form and structure to the garden.

GROWING NOTES

Lirope is easy to grow. It requires well-drained soil in sun or shade and needs extra water during dry periods. Divide the clumps in early spring. Plants that are tatty can be cut back and fertilized in spring to encourage strong new growth.

MISCANTHUS SINENSIS
MISCANTHUS

Miscanthus not only looks good, it's also a useful plant to have around the garden. As most species of this attractive ornamental grass are tall growing, they can be used to mask other plants or hide parts of the garden. The large form grows to 2–3 metres (6–10 ft) and the smaller varieties reach to 75 cm (30 inches) high. Miscanthus comes in a wide range of forms, too—some have fine, narrow leaves, producing a graceful clump, others are coarse or have variegated or patterned leaves. In autumn and winter, the leaves become straw-like. Most species also have attractive flowers and seed heads. The popular 'Silver Feather' (or 'Silberfeder') has silvery pink flowers on slender stems, 'Zebrinus' or zebra grass, has splashes of gold across its leaves and 'Variegatus' features striped, cream-and-green leaves.

With miscanthus you can hide a multitude of sins and have a showy plant at the same time. Popular forms include the gold-splashed 'Zebrinus' (opposite and top left); cream-and-green-striped 'Variegatus' (top centre); and the pink-flowered 'Silver Feather' (top right).

GROWING NOTES

Miscanthus likes sun and soil that is well drained but moist. Fuel the tall growth by digging in plenty of well-rotted organic matter when planting. Cut the plants down in early spring and fertilize; divide the larger clumps in winter.

NARCISSUS SPECIES
NARCISSUS, DAFFODIL, JONQUIL

For a burst of exuberant seasonal colour, the ever-popular narcissus is well worth a look. This vibrant group includes sunny jonquils, fragrant paper whites and glorious daffodils. From late autumn in warm climates, when the yellow jonquils bloom, narcissus forms clumps of narrow strappy leaves studded with flowers. Plant a range of narcissus for a spectacular flower show through to summer. Narcissus will naturalize under deciduous trees or just pop in a few clumps as focal points in a flower garden or a pot.

GROWING NOTES

Narcissus needs sun and well-drained soil, but select the best species for your climate. Jonquils thrive in warm and cool climates, while daffodils are best in cool to cold climates. All species enjoy sun in cool areas and some shade in warmer areas. The key to success in growing narcissus is to allow the leaves to die back naturally. Water and feed regularly from when plants begin to flower until the leaves die down. Leave bulbs to naturalize in most gardens but lift and store daffodils where soils are wet or summers are very hot and humid.

Since William Wordsworth immortalized the 'host of golden daffodils' in his poetry, gardeners have aspired to create their own golden fields by mass-planting narcissus. This bright and cheerful plant also works wonders under deciduous trees.

OPHIOPOGON JAPONICUS
MONDO GRASS

Mondo grass is a wonderful plant for a low-maintenance garden. It's hardy, grows quickly and lasts forever. Growing in a strappy clump to 30–60 cm (12–24 inches) high and wide, it makes an effective low-growing edging plant for flower beds, paving or paths or as a border between shrubbery and a lawn. It can also be used as an alternative to a formal lawn. It doesn't need mowing and gives a lush, green look all year round. If access is required, use stepping stones to make an informal pathway through the greenery. Dwarf forms, which only reach to 5–10 cm (2–4 inches) in height, fit nicely between pavers where they can be used to outline each paver or create a visual break that will soften a large space. Alternatively, use the dwarf form to create interesting patterns. Make a chequerboard effect with rows or diagonal bands of mondo grass interspersed with gravel, pebbles or recycled

One of the easiest and quickest ways to soften the edges of a pathway is to grow clumps of mondo grass. You'll also be rewarded with lush green foliage all year round.

Although grown mainly for its lush, low foliage, mondo grass produces flowers and decorative berries amid its leaves. A gravel pathway flanked by clumps of dwarf mondo grass provides wonderful contrasting textures.

glass. Ribbons of mondo can also divide areas of groundcover plants. These patterns are most effective when viewed from above. Dwarf or mini mondo forms are equally impressive. For a complete colour change, try the slow-growing black mondo, *O. planiscapus* 'Nigrescens', which has purple-black leaves. This cultivar looks dramatic when grown with burgundy or silvery foliage plants such as ajuga or artemesia. Highlight the black colour with light-coloured gravel or mulch.

GROWING NOTES

Mondo grass grows in sun or light shade in well-drained soil. Although drought tolerant, plants will burn if conditions are hot and dry. During dry periods, provide regular deep water around the base of the plants. For strong leafy growth, keep plants well watered and fertilize at least annually. Plants naturally form a dense clump and can be divided as required.

PHORMIUM COOKIANUM AND *P. TENAX*
NEW ZEALAND FLAX

New Zealand flax makes a striking focal point in the garden nestled in among colourful, low-growing plants. It also works well as a single specimen in a pot.

If you ever wanted to make a statement with just one plant, New Zealand flax will do it. This hardy plant is valued for its dramatic appeal with its bold clump of long, narrow arching leaves. It comes in a range of sizes from 60 cm (2 ft) to 150 cm (5ft) high. Highlight its splendour by surrounding it with gravel, a low groundcover or a combination of succulents and ornamental grasses. Leaf colours are amazing, too—browns, reds, copper, burgundy and all hues of a sunset as well as variegated forms with stripes of green, gold and cream. Plants bloom in summer, producing long-lasting tall spires of bird-attracting flowers. New Zealand flax also thrives in pots, but select dwarf forms, such as 'Duet', when planting in containers.

GROWING NOTES
New Zealand flax is a highly adaptable plant and does well in coastal gardens. It will grow in sun or light shade, and is frost hardy. Flax tolerates drought but looks best in a moist, well-watered soil. Divide the large clumps in spring when necessary. Prune to remove spent flower stems and tatty foliage.

TULBAGHIA VIOLACEA
SOCIETY GARLIC

With its dainty flowers on long stems and dense, grey-green foliage, society garlic is a visual delight. It also has a garlic-like odour! It was so named during Victorian times when it was used in place of garlic. Apparently, it didn't taint the breath as did garlic and so was considered more socially acceptable! This leafy clump, reaching to 30 cm (12 inches) tall, has 40 cm- (16 inch-) long stems that bear pretty violet to white flowers. While the leaves of most species are grey-green, those of the variegated form, 'Silver Lace', are edged in white. Use society garlic as an evergreen edge to a garden bed or plant clumps among perennials to extend flower interest into summer. Plants can also be grown in pots. This plant is a good choice for a coastal garden.

GROWING NOTES

If society garlic is given full sun and moist soil, particularly in spring and early summer, it will produce a strong plant with lots of flowers. While it can withstand moderate frost, it doesn't do well in cold, wet soils. Plants tolerate light shade in warm climates. Divide clumps in spring or early summer.

Picture-perfect and robust, *Tulbaghia violacea* looks good as a border plant, in a rockery or garden bed and even in a container.

WATSONIA SPECIES
WATSONIA

The long-flowering watsonia gives colour and interest in a spring garden well into summer. Some species also flower into winter. The plant has a tall, striking, leafy clump punctuated in spring and summer with spires of white, pink or apricot flowers on strong stems. A clump can be 1.5–2 metres (5–6 ft) tall in full flower, making it an ideal accent plant for a sunny garden. Watsonia looks spectacular contrasted with fine, rounded plants such as wormwood or lavender. The dwarf varieties are ideal for planting in confined spaces or in pots.

GROWING NOTES

Watsonia grows easily from corms planted in autumn, and rapidly develops into a large clump. It grows best in full sun with well-drained soil but some species tolerate shade. Others thrive in moist conditions. They will tolerate only light frost. Lift and divide large clumps every two to three years. In some areas, watsonias are weedy and should not be grown near bushland or natural watercourses. Remove spent flowers and seed heads to prevent plants from self-seeding.

Watsonia is flower power. It has gorgeous spires of blooms with an amazing range of colours and bold and handsome foliage.

ZEPHYRANTHES CANDIDA
RAIN LILY

The versatile rain lily performs well in a border, in pockets of a rockery and even under trees and shrubs, providing colour from summer to autumn.

The rain lily is an ideal warm-climate plant, offering starry, cup-shaped flowers on long stems and lush, dark green foliage. This vigorous species grows to around 15 cm (6 inches) tall. Flowers are single-stemmed in white or lilac-pink with prominent yellow stamens and its leaves are evergreen and reed-like. The rain lily flowers from late summer to autumn, usually after heavy summer rain. This plant can be used in a variety of ways—as an edging plant or massed in clumps to soften a rockery or to add contrast among succulents. It's also a good choice for a flowering evergreen border. In cold areas, grow rain lilies in pots in a greenhouse. A potted rain lily also makes a striking table decoration.

GROWING NOTES

Rain lilies are grown from bulbs or by dividing an established clump. Once planted, they establish readily and need little extra care. They thrive in a sunny, well-drained spot in fertile soil and flower best when kept well watered in summer. Plants may die back in frosty and cold climates.

grasses

The grass you grow doesn't have to be the grass you mow. Welcome to the world of ornamental grasses, home to some of nature's top performers. These easy-care plants have elegant, arching forms, a range of glorious colours and are versatile—they can be used as a feature, edging, border, massed planting or potted specimen. They also come in a range of sizes to suit all landscapes.

Grasses have a lot going for them. Their rich tapestries of colours, textures and forms bring drama, beauty and structure to the garden. And their sizes are virtually made to order—ranging from low, tufty plants, such as festucas, to tall clumps several metres (3 ft or more) high, such as miscanthus or stipa. Many species of grasses are evergreen, some have seasonal colour, and others produce long-lasting flowers and seed heads. On the practical side, ornamental grasses have become popular plants for landscapers and garden designers because of their no-fuss growth habit, pest and disease resistance and drought, heat and cold tolerance.

Grasses can be planted in gardens as tall clumps to make a statement or form a focal point in a massed garden planting or along a vista. Tall species can also be used to conceal what lies beyond. A simple but effective way to use grasses is massed together. Plant a selection of different species with varying heights and spreads. If grasses are being grown in containers, grow them in pots of different heights to add to the impact.

Grasses team well with many garden plants. They give striking contrast when combined with low and spreading

Previous page: The hardy *Carex* species comes in a wide range of coloured and variegated foliage. Clockwise from top left: Fountain grass; variegated sedge; zebra grass (in winter); and foxtail barley.

Japanese blood grass (*Imperata cyclindrica* 'Rubra') is one of the most vibrantly coloured ornamental grasses. Its handsome, green foliage turns brilliant red from late summer into autumn.

plants such as succulents and flowering perennials. The fine, ribbon-like leaves of grasses are a counterpoint to large, lush foliage plants like hostas or daylilies. For a modern, minimalist look, combine a small clumping grass, such as the silver-blue *Festuca glauca*, with coloured pebbles or recycled glass.

One of the best ways to use grasses in gardens is to position them where they can be viewed with the light behind them, particularly the late-afternoon sun. Rays of sunlight transform a grassy clump or a seed head into a living sculpture that glows with warmth and colour, even in the depths of winter. In cold-winter gardens grasses sparkle on a frosty morning as they're caught by rays of early morning sun.

Fountain grass (*Pennisetum* spp.) with its cylindrical flowers, has some of the best seed heads. Many pennisetums are called foxtails because of their thick tail-like seed heads, which develop red or claret tones. The tall-growing *Stipa gigantea* also has large and impressive seed heads. The zebra grasses, such as *Miscanthus sinensis*, hold their plumes of seeds well into winter.

Grasses can also be used to introduce movement into a garden. Grasses sway and ripple in the gentlest breeze. When

the wind gets blustery they bend and bow but are not likely to be damaged or broken. Some will even sing, murmur or sigh as the breeze blows through them, bringing the dimension of sound to the garden.

Grasses will surprise with their colour range. The new growth of Japanese blood grass, *Imperata cylindrica*, features a spectacular mix of vibrant bright red and lime-green as it pokes its way through the soil in spring. Also offering long leafy clumps of colour are the attractive *Carex* species. Colours can range from gold, yellow, cream and white to the deep russet tones of *C. buchananii*. There are many named varieties of carex, each selected for its colour, size or leaf shape, which can be straight or curly.

Grasses add movement and foliage contrast. Clockwise from top left: Blue fescue; reddish-brown sedge; light-brown sedge; and variegated zebra grass.

GROWING NOTES

Grasses are easy to grow, both in the garden and in containers. Most species like full sun and well-drained soil. Some tolerate dry conditions but others, particularly reeds and rushes, need moist soil. Herbaceous species are best suited to cooler areas while evergreens grow in warm areas (some will grow in cooler

The late-afternoon sun illuminates the elegant, arching foliage and tall, feathery flower heads of these clumps of grasses. A magical display like this is easily achieved by positioning plants where they will be backlit by the sun's rays.

areas as well). Encourage strong growth on all species with extra water in spring when most grasses are sending up new leaves. Make early spring the time to give grasses a generous feed of fertilizer. Protect their roots with a layer of organic mulch, pebbles or gravel. As the season progresses and plants mature, flower and set seed, they will generally survive with less water, even during dry periods.

Grasses can be annual, which means they'll grow, bloom, seed and die down over one or two seasons, or perennial, which means they grow over several years. Annual grasses are grown from seed or replanted each year like bedding plants. Some species self-seed, reliably reshooting year after year.

Prune perennial grasses when they become untidy and the herbaceous when they begin to die down in late summer or autumn. Where perennial grasses willingly hold their leaves during the cold winter months, leave them unpruned until the end of winter. Then, in early spring, cut them back hard to the ground to make room for the strong, new growth.

No matter the number of plants we have in our garden, invariably there are always pockets of blank space. These bare patches of earth are unsightly, and a haven for weeds. The obvious solution, of course, is to mulch the troublespots. But there is a more attractive option, and it comes in the form of lovely living carpets—groundcovers, mounding

Make an undulating effect with a carpet that combines a lush, dense groundcover and mounding plants.
Previous pages: Carpet plants, like these sweet violets, have the bonus of lightly perfumed flowers.

and climbing plants. As well as covering a bare area, carpet plants bring the wonders of colour, texture and contrast into the garden. Many also offer fragrance.

Carpet plants soften the edges of paths, paving and steps, provide luxuriant fill around a rockery or bare spot and create a thick blanket over a brick wall. We unroll some top-brand carpets for your perusal.

Succulents with rosette shapes make a dense carpet either alone or combined with other foliage plants. Following pages: A lawn forms a lush carpet in the garden.

Top: Ajuga comes in foliage colours from green to bronze, burgundy or multicoloured like this variegated form, called 'Spanish Lace'.
Opposite: As the name suggests, 'Metallica Crispa' has a lovely metallic sheen.

AJUGA REPTANS
AJUGA, BUGLE

Ajuga carpets the ground with lush, vigorous growth and small spires of flowers that last from spring to summer. Use it to border along a path, soften paving, or as cover underneath taller plants such as standard roses. It is most often seen with green leaves and blue flowers, but there are cultivars with coloured and textured leaves that can introduce year-round interest to a planting scheme. 'Jungle Bronze' has wavy bronze leaves while 'Burgundy Glow' has greenish leaves tinged with red. Some varieties have been selected for the colour or height of their flowers. For a really impressive carpet, 'Caitlin's Giant' has exceptionally tall, deep-mauve flower spires up to 15 cm (6 inches) high.

GROWING NOTES
Ajuga grows in any soil or situation but is best in a sunny, well-drained spot. A little bit can go a long way so keep this carpet controlled at the edges. Ajuga will spread to cover 120 cm (48 inches) or more. It can grow 10–20 cm (4–8 inches) tall.

ARMERIA MARITIMA
THRIFT

Pretty yet hardy, thrift is the carpet plant for a harsh, seaside environment. This tough plant produces dense, tufty leaves that form a thick mat 20–30 cm (8–12 inches) high even in areas that are constantly whipped by salt and winds. Thrift's ability to thrive in such harsh conditions has given rise to its common name. Flower colours are mostly brilliant pink but some forms have white blooms. The attractive forest of flowers stands well above the blue-green leafy tufts. One of the attractions of thrift is its dense growth, particularly in hot, dry rockeries or seaside gardens so this plant will turn bare into beautiful. Team it with spiky rockery plants, silver foliage plants or brilliant ice plants.

GROWING NOTES

Thrift does quite literally thrive on neglect, but it must have full sun and very well-drained soil to be seen at its best. Deadhead spent flowers to encourage growth.

Thrift makes a cushiony carpet in a rock garden or near the seaside.

CAMPANULA PORTENSCHLAGIANA
BELLFLOWER

The robust bellflower can form mounds up to 30 cm (12 inches) high and has an indefinite spread. *C. poscharskyana* (above) has small, star-like flowers and those of *C. portenschlagiana* (opposite) are bell shaped.

The dainty groundcover bellflowers have more than their fair share of difficult Latin names but they are not hard to grow. *C. portenschlagiana* is a beautiful groundcover plant massed with tiny, mauve-blue bells from late spring. It reaches 15 cm (6 inches) high and spreads well, even over rocks and edges and among shrubs. However, this plant does not become invasive. The closely related *C. poscharskyana* is similar, but with blue-mauve, star-shaped flowers. There are named varieties with coloured flowers such as 'Lisduggan Variety' (pink), 'Multiplicity' (double mauve) and 'E.H. Frost' (white). Flowering is most prolific in summer and can extend into autumn.

GROWING NOTES
The groundcover bellflowers come from the Northern Hemisphere and prefer cool to mild climates and well-drained soil. They are grown in full sun to part shade and are frost tolerant. Water well in dry spells.

CERASTIUM TOMENTOSUM
SNOW-IN-SUMMER

hile snow-in-summer's common name comes from the masses of tiny white flowers that cover it in summer, this carpeting plant's true value lies in its year-round, grey-green leaves and soft growth. It moulds itself over steps, rocks or garden edges, or sits like a thick rug beside a path. It will spread quickly so it is efficient at choking out weeds and gives instant softness to a new planting. It can be used in pots, window boxes or a hanging basket. It makes a fine companion for roses or perennials and softens a rockery. Snow-in-summer also enjoys a spot in a seaside garden. Plants reach 10–15 cm (4–6 inches) high and spread 60–90 cm (24–36 inches).

Snow-in-summer is a great choice where a soft, gentle element is needed such as in a hot rock garden or in a newly planted garden.

GROWING NOTES

Snow-in-summer must have sun and good drainage. This plant enjoys dry conditions and can take heat and cold. Clip it after flowering to restore its pristine foliage. If it spreads too much, give it a few cuts from a sharp spade or trowel.

CHAMAEMELUM NOBILE
CHAMOMILE

Chamomile is popular worldwide when made into a cup of tea, but this dainty herb has a lot more going for it. For starters, this groundcover has lovely, fern-like green leaves and cute-as-a-button daisy flowers from late spring to early autumn. In cool to cold climates chamomile is also a popular alternative to lawn—the non-flowering 'Treneague' is ideal. Chamomile can also drape over walls or grow among stepping stones and the bonus is the fragrance it emits when it is crushed or walked on. Both the flowers and leaves are used for brewing tea. Plants grow around 10–30 cm (4–12 inches) high and spread to at least 30 cm (12 inches) in diameter.

Enjoy the spicy apple fragrance of chamomile as an alternative to lawn or simply grow as a clump in the herb garden.

GROWING NOTES

Chamomile prefers an open area and a light, sandy soil for good drainage. In hotter and more humid climates it is best grown as a clump in an airy spot, as plants are often too elongated or short-lived to form a lawn.

COTONEASTER HORIZONTALIS
COTONEASTER

The prostrate cotoneaster, *C. horizontalis* has long-lasting appeal. Treasure this low shrub for its long, flat branches, all neatly attired in deep-green, shiny leaves. Rejoice in its ability to grow on any surface, horizontal or vertical. Train it to cascade over a low wall, run down the edge of steps or use it as mantle or drape. Even allow it to grow as an espalier along a fence or wall. This cotoneaster is easy to train and shape, making it a good beginner's plant. The red berries, which are long lasting, bring colour to the garden in winter. In most cool to temperate climates cotoneaster is evergreen, but in very cold climates it may become deciduous through autumn and winter.

The versatile *Cotoneaster horizontalis* can be spread, draped or shaped to suit a variety of garden designs.

GROWING NOTES

This cotoneaster is not fussy about soil or aspect, but berry production is best in a sunny spot. Once established, it is tolerant of dry conditions but will grow better with regular watering. Prune in spring and train to maintain its shape.

DIANTHUS SPECIES
DIANTHUS, CARNATIONS, PINKS

Dianthus have flat, open or many-petalled flowers that delight with their clove-like scent and lovely colour.

If gorgeous fluffy colour is your desire, dianthus comes up trumps. And the range of plants is extensive, including carnations, pinks and sweet Williams. The best choice for a carpet effect are the pinks; these old-fashioned dianthus have tufted growth, compact, blue-green leaves and sweetly scented pink, red or white flowers. These plants make an excellent border along a sunny path and form a soft, fragrant edging to a flower garden. They are a traditional choice in a cottage garden or can bring colour to a herb or kitchen garden. Dianthus come from the Mediterranean region so grow well in any garden with this type of climate. For large, showy flowers for picking, look for a carnation (*Dianthus caryophyllus*), which may have stems of single flowers or sprays of smaller blooms.

GROWING NOTES

Dianthus are lime-loving plants. In acid soils, add lime and well-rotted compost when preparing a garden area for planting. They also require full sun and good drainage. Protect the root system with a generous layer of organic mulch.

DICHONDRA REPENS
DICHONDRA, KIDNEY WEED

When a large, green area is called for in the garden, the ground-hugging dichondra is an excellent choice. Unlike lawn, which is high maintenance, dichondra requires only sun and water. It has small, green, kidney-shaped leaves and forms a low dense cover. This perennial also works well around stepping stones, in confined or narrow spaces or in shady spots under trees. It can be planted to form patterns and shapes, particularly around pathways. Dichondra suits a wild or low-maintenance, informal garden.

The densely packed leaves of dichondra make it a soft lawn, lush groundcover or a softening element between stepping stones.

GROWING NOTES

Dichondra can be grown from seed or from plugs or runners. It grows to less than 25 mm (1 inch) high so doesn't need mowing. It grows best in a temperate, frost-free climate in shade or semi-shade and tolerates poor drainage. Water deeply in spring and summer for lush growth.

GAZANIA X HYBRIDA
GAZANIA, TREASURE FLOWER

Gazanias flower for most of the year and can be massed for a low-maintenance carpet.

Harsh, exposed areas do not mean a dull garden—not when you can plant a carpet of gorgeous gazanias. These groundcovering perennials have bright and cheerful, daisy-like flowers in red, orange, mahogany, cream and pink, often with contrasting stripes or centres. Their low rosette of foliage acts as a foil to the bright flowers and forms the practical service of holding together soil on slopes, banks or areas where grass can't grow. Gazanias give bold colour along a driveway or path. Where a driveway consists of a pair of concrete tracks, a planting of gazanias along the centre softens the look and ties the drive into its surroundings. Gazanias also thrive near the sea, or on a sunny, wind-swept balcony in a pot or container.

GROWING NOTES

Gazanias grow in all warm climates, including tropical and arid areas. They require little water and are unfussy about soil type, but it should be well drained. They do need full sun—the flowers of most gazanias only fully open on sunny days.

HEDERA HELIX
IVY

Ivy can be trained into a wreath shape or used as a carpet between trees or shaded paving. Never let ivy grow up a trunk as it will damage the tree.

It is often said that ivy is a good servant but a bad master. So, if you're not into regular maintenance and don't enjoy pruning, think twice about ivy. Left unchecked it invades trees, climbs walls, scurries into bushland and generally gets out of control. With regular pruning—from a lawn mower if it's a groundcover plant or shears if it is growing on a wall—ivy is a useful and versatile carpet plant. It loves shade, grows happily between trees and can be clipped into almost any shape. It comes in green and variegated tones in a range of decorative and dainty leaf shapes.

GROWING NOTES
Ivy is unfussy about soil conditions but is best in shade. This frost-hardy species requires regular hard pruning. To prune or cut out, first hose the plant down. Then cover your face with a mask and wear protective clothing to protect yourself from allergy-causing dust and mites.

HETEROCENTRON ELEGANS
SPANISH SHAWL

Showy Spanish shawl is a popular groundcover in warm-climate areas. It produces masses of cerise-coloured flowers which adorn the plant from spring to summer. As a carpeting plant, however, colour is only one of its virtues. It has a very flat growth habit, only 8–10 cm (3–4 inches) high but will spread to 100 cm (40 inches). This flat, but spreading, habit is evident where it is allowed to drape over a wall or fall from a hanging basket. It can also be grown as a dense, long-lived groundcover. Team it with large foliage plants such as palms for a neat, trim contrast as well as seasonal colour. Spanish shawl can also be grown between paving stones or beside a path and performs well in a container.

GROWING NOTES

The slow-growing Spanish shawl rarely becomes troublesome or invasive. It prefers a warm, humid climate and must be given a frost-free spot with good drainage. It grows well in both sun or dappled shade.

Spanish shawl makes a spectacular groundcover, especially when contrasted with green foliage plants. It can also be used to cover a wall, providing a curtain of bold colour from spring to summer.

JUNIPERUS CONFERTA
SHORE JUNIPER

While conifers are often considered to be large trees, there are some that hug the ground to form attractive and long-lived groundcover plants. One of the most useful is the shore juniper, *Juniperus conferta*. This plant forms a dense, prickly, horizontal mass. It can spread 3–4 metres (10–12 ft), growing around 1 metre (3 ft) a year, and will form a low mound 50 cm (20 inches) high. It is useful as a groundcover or barrier in any harsh environment such as near the sea, in dry or sandy soils, or on a hot exposed embankment. The foliage is dense, making it a good groundcover and barrier against weeds. It will also trail over walls or beside steps. It is prickly so should not be used where it will be brushed against. It has an aromatic scent when crushed.

Top: The bright-green, evergreen foliage of the shore juniper is a great contrast to a wall. Above: Also prostrate is the closely related *Juniperus squamata*.

GROWING NOTES

Although not for the tropics, shore juniper will thrive in most climates and is particularly good near the coast. This fast-growing plant needs little pruning other than the removal of wayward shoots from time to time.

LAMIUM MACULATUM
DEAD NETTLE

Showy on all fronts, dead nettle is a vigorous grower that works well as a groundcover or potted plant. It looks magnificent in a hanging basket, too.

Despite its ugly common name, dead nettle looks good all year round. This attractive evergreen has dainty flowers in soft mauves, pinks and white. Some species have yellow flowers. The leaves can range from green to almost metallic silver with splashes of white or cream, so when planting to lighten or brighten a shaded area, select a variety with attractively marked foliage. Dead nettle is seen at its best in a moist, shaded garden where it fills in among shrubs or cascades over the edges of garden beds or paths. This vigorous groundcover will form roots (stolons) as it grows so it can spread 2 metres (6 ft) or more. It can also be grown in a container.

GROWING NOTES

Dead nettle grows best in a mild to warm climate but will not tolerate the tropics. It prefers a shaded position and although tolerant of a wide range of soils, it will grow and flower best with well-drained soil that's rich in organic matter.

LAMPRANTHUS SPECIES
ICE PLANT

En masse, ice plants are electric. When planting an open area with these flowering succulents, team them with other sun-loving plants, such as daisies and gazanias, for foliage and flower contrast.

Get out the sunglasses when the ice plant is in flower because you'll need them. The mass of iridescent flowers that covers ice plants in late winter and spring has a vibrancy that's rarely seen in the plant world. In full bloom, the flowers are so densely massed that they completely cover the plant's succulent leaves. And they come in an array of dazzling colours—purple, red, magenta, pink, yellow and white.

The sheer strength of their flower colour can make ice plants difficult to use in a landscape where colours are refined or muted but, where exciting and stimulating informal planting is your desire, let them take over. These hardy plants can be massed to form a boldly patterned carpet or teamed with other sun-lovers, such as gazanias, for year-round colour. They are ideal choices for a rockery or to plant a low-maintenance area beside the sea. They can also be used to create colourful, seasonal flowering interest in a succulent or cactus garden. When ice plants are not in bloom, the grey-green leaves make a tough, long-lasting groundcover.

Ice plants are also great beginners' plants. With their fast growth, ease of propagation (they'll grow very easily from a

cutting) and exceptional flowering they are hard to beat as a way to cover large, bare new gardens or brighten up dark spots.

Ice plants are just one of a group of trailing succulents that tolerate dry, harsh, sun-drenched conditions. *Lampranthus aureus*, *L. roseus* and *L. spectabilis* make wonderful groundcovers and can be used to stabilize soil—even sand.

Colour doesn't get any bolder and brighter than this. When the ice plant is not in bloom, its grey-green leaves provide a tough groundcover.

GROWING NOTES

Plant and stand back is about all the direction that's needed for these plants. They enjoy full sun and tolerate wind, poor soils and, once established, get by on very little extra water. Ice plants are best in warm to hot climates. They will not survive extremely cold or wet winters. In cold climates ice plants can be grown in pots and given glasshouse protection over winter.

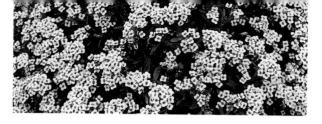

LOBULARIA MARITIMA

ALYSSUM, SWEET ALICE

Alyssum, with its tiny, white, pink or mauve flowers is one of the prettiest carpet plants. It is also a fast-growing plant. Although it is grown as an annual it can last several seasons. Use alyssum in the garden as a soft, unifying edging to a massed floral display or to soften the edges of steps or garden beds. Where there are areas of hot paving, alyssum can be used around the edges or between pavers like a flowering cushion. Rounded and compact, this plant grows 20–25 cm (8–10 inches) high and up to 20–45 cm (8–15 inches) wide. It will also happily trail over the edge of a container. Alyssum is an excellent choice to plant around the edge of a potted standard or to fill a window box or hanging basket.

GROWING NOTES

Alyssum thrives in any climate, likes full sun and tolerates any well-drained soil. It can be grown from seed or seedling. It will also happily self-sow, particularly into cracks and crevices beside paths or among paving. Deadhead after flowering.

Alyssum is quick-growing, with flowering starting within eight weeks after sowing. Masses of pretty blooms last from late spring to late summer.

MENTHA SPECIES
MINT

F ast-growing, aromatic and prolific, mint is often overlooked as a groundcover plant. It especially works well in shaded and moist areas. Best known is the culinary spearmint, *Mentha spicata*, which is one of the few herbs that doesn't need full sun. For soft foliage it's hard to beat the vigorous, apple-scented *M. suaveolens*. The variegated form, 'Variegata', has white-and-green leaves and a fruity fragrance. Eau-de-cologne mint (*M. x piperita*) is a taller-growing species with glossy green leaves. Popular pennyroyal (*M. pulegium*) is an excellent, no-fuss groundcover. It has large, slightly aromatic bright-green leaves and creeping stems. It can be used around stepping stones in sunny to partially shaded areas or as a groundcover among shrubs and perennials.

Many species of mint make effective groundcovers. However, they can be invasive. Different varieties have different aromas, including apple and eau-de-cologne as well as the popular peppermint and spearmint.

GROWING NOTES

Mint thrives in any moist soil in sun or partial shade. It spreads by runners and quickly forms a dense mat. Most species are frost hardy. Mint can be invasive, but can be contained with paving. Spearmint can also be grown in containers.

PRATIA SPECIES
PRATIA

Pratia forms a lush, living mat of soft, bright-green leaves. The spreading stems with tiny, toothed leaves are densely packed so this ground-hugging plant forms a thick, weed-suppressing cover. The growth is extremely dainty and, in spring through summer, the plant is studded with starry flowers in white, blue or mauve. Pratia can be used as a green carpet around stepping stones or informal pathways, but it doesn't tolerate heavy foot traffic. In a shaded courtyard, pratia will soften harsh paving. It can also be grown as a living mulch for potted plants and is particularly effective when allowed to cascade gently over the sides.

Pratia forms a dense, soft carpet in a wide range of climates. A bonus is the pretty, star-shaped flowers, usually white or pale blue.

GROWING NOTES
Despite its delicate appearance, pratia is frost hardy. It grows in full sun to partial shade but prefers a moist, freely draining soil. Give it extra water in summer to keep the growth lush, but hold back during winter. If it spreads further than you wish, simply sever the excess growth with a spade.

THYMUS SPECIES

THYME

There are more than 300 species of thyme and all come with a delightful fragrance. This hardy plant works well as a sun-loving groundcover, around rockeries or paving stones or carpeting a bank.

Thyme's aromatic leaves exude a wonderful perfume, especially on hot, still days or when they are crushed under foot. Most species are creeping plants that grow happily in cracks of paving, carpeting rockeries or sprawling across a sunny garden bed. They have pretty flowers in white, pink or mauve and leaves can be variegated or golden. Creeping thyme (*Thymus serpyllum*) is tough enough to take light foot traffic so is a good choice where a groundcover plant will be trodden on. Thyme looks especially attractive when it is surrounded by different types of gravel or crushed stone. A particularly appealing plant is the lemon-scented *T. x citriodorus*, which can be grown in the herb garden, in pots or as a groundcover. Most species will grow to a height of 30 cm (12 inches).

GROWING NOTES

Thyme loves hot, dry and sunny conditions of a Mediterranean climate but thrives in all but humid and tropical zones. It enjoys a moist, well-drained soil. Plants last for several years, but should be renewed when they become woody. For thick, dense plants, remove the flower heads after flowering.

TRACHELOSPERMUM JASMINOIDES
STAR JASMINE

Star jasmine is a star in every sense of the word. This spectacularly beautiful plant makes a wonderful climbing specimen (over a fence, trellis or archway) or a lush, foliage groundcover or it can be trimmed into a hedge or into interesting shapes such as a standard or topiary. It also works a treat in containers. As star jasmine performs well in both sun and shade it is a useful plant to visually tie gardens together, from all areas of the landscape. It has glossy, evergreen leaves and clusters of strongly perfumed white flowers. In spring, when this plant is in full bloom, the scent is overwhelming. Expect spot flowers at other times. The variegated form, 'Tricolor', is grown for its striking pink-and-cream foliage.

GROWING NOTES

Although tolerant of sun and shade and soils ranging from dry to moist, flowering is best on plants that are grown in full sun, in rich, well-drained soils. Once established, plants are fairly drought tolerant. Shear off extra growth in summer.

Star jasmine will soften bare areas whether it is grown as a curtain or carpet. The starry flowers are intensely fragrant.

VINCA MINOR
PERIWINKLE

Easy-care periwinkle is a popular carpeting plant that's ideal for decorating difficult areas in the garden. This evergreen creeper has densely packed, glossy, green leaves and attractive lilac-blue flowers that appear in spring. Particularly appealing is the variegated form which has deep-green leaves edged with cream. Periwinkle spreads readily, forming roots at each node. While this encourages a dense groundcover it may also lead the plant to becoming invasive, especially in warm climates. Keep it contained and limit its spread with pruning. It is good for shaded areas under trees, on banks, in large rockeries or in low-maintenance areas. The larger-leaved form, *Vinca major*, can be invasive and should be avoided.

Periwinkle makes a lush groundcover and contrasts well with other foliage plants. The variegated form (top) provides foliage colour all year round.

GROWING NOTES
Periwinkle is easy to grow in most conditions but does best in well-drained soil enriched with organic matter, like manure. It thrives in sun or shade and, once established, is drought tolerant. To keep growth thick and dense, especially in heavy shade or where there is root competition, give extra water.

VIOLA HEDERACEA, V. ODORATA
VIOLETS

Violets are pretty plants but not all are grown for their fragrant flowers. The Australian violet, *Viola hederacea*, excels as a groundcover carpet in moist, shaded gardens. Its dainty leaves, which are almost circular in shape, form a lush green carpet. In spring and summer, the plant is a mass of tiny white-and-mauve-violet flowers, held above the leaves on slender stalks. Athough lacking the scent of its European relatives, the Australian violet is captivating. It is an ideal choice for a lawn substitute in moist shade in narrow passageways, or near water. It is also a good choice for a small courtyard or a garden with a Japanese theme. Where it is likely to be trodden on, place stepping stones to make a path. These protect the plant and also the moist soil it loves to grow in.

The Australian violet is attractive spilling from a container in a shaded garden and makes an excellent groundcover grown among ferns, azaleas, camellias and other shade-loving plants.

The sweet violet, *V. odorata*, suits a very different situation. This is a plant to grow in the sun and to relish for its richly

Not all violets are the same. *V. odorata* (above) has intensely fragrant flowers and loves the sun and a cool climate. The non-fragrant *V. hederacea* (opposite) needs a moist, shady spot.

If *Viola odorata* (above) gets too much shade it will produce few or no flowers. The pretty, violet-and-white blooms of *V. hederacea* make a colourful carpet under spreading trees and other shaded areas.

fragrant flowers and heart-shaped leaves. Best known for their deep purple flowers, sweet violets come in a range of flower colours including pink, white and burgundy violet. Some are also bicolour and there are double forms. The sweet violet is a traditional cottage garden plant grown beside a path to bring colour and fragrance in winter and spring.

GROWING NOTES

These violets need very different growing situations. The Australian violet needs moist, shaded conditions. It spreads gently and rarely becomes invasive but can be controlled by limiting water or by digging it up where it is not wanted. In contrast, the sweet violet loves full sun and rich, fertile, well-drained soil. Deep watering is recommended, particularly to promote flowering. Plants can be cut back in autumn to make way for new growth and flowers.

soft
edges

Straight lines have a place in garden design, providing structure and form. But sometimes, they can be ugly—too formal, stark or hard—and can detract from the overall beauty of the garden. The solution is to use plants to soften those hard edges, to blur the lines a little and perhaps add elements of colour, texture and scent along the way. Here are our suggestions for a soft touch.

One of the best subjects for softening edges is a set of steps. A simple planting of trailing or softly cascading plants, such as ivy, convolvulus, plectranthrus or star jasmine (*Trachelospermum jasminoides*), along each side can transform an area, replacing the hard lines of the steps with soft, lush foliage or a mass of beautiful flowers.

If you are building steps, allow for a narrow strip of soil along the junction of each step riser and tread to grow bands of softening plants. Plants that grow well in this way include ivy, box honeysuckle (*Lonicera nitida*), and star jasmine, all of which can be clipped into the desired shape. For an informal band around steps, try dwarf mondo grass or the dainty seaside daisy.

Where there are paths or paving next to garden beds, there are endless possibilities for creating the look you want. In formal designs, a simple and continuous edging of a structural plant, such as mondo grass, enhances the formality while still softening the hard line of a path's edge.

To maintain a unified planting scheme but with less rigidity, use a continuous edging row of a gently sprawling or flowering plant such as dianthus, arabis or even dwarf lavender. If casual

Previous page: Hard walls can be softened in so many ways with plants like these gazanias that spill, sprawl or cascade.

Opposite: Plain steps become charming features when plants are used to enhance their shape or soften their outlines. Use foliage plants such as ivy in shade, or the pretty seaside daisy (*Erigeron*) in hot spots.

A border of edging plants enhances the shape of a sweeping lawn, especially when the plants contrast in colour and texture.

and natural is your look, then go for a selection of different plants along the edge, mixing heights, textures and colours.

The same principles apply for the edge between a sweep of lawn and a garden bed. A continuous edging plant helps to accentuate the shape of the lawn and adds a level of structure and formality. Choose plants that provide contrast to the lawn through foliage colour or flowers and avoid any that will grow too vigorously over the lawn.

Retaining walls can look harsh and imposing, but are ideal places to showcase flowering and perfumed spillover plants. For high walls, choose a plant that can trail for the required distance, such as trailing convolvulus (*Convolvulus sabatius*), trailing lantana (*Lantana montevidensis* and its cultivars), and the many and varied ivies, which all trail 150 cm (60 inches) or more. Plants that are usually vigorous climbers, such as the perfumed star jasmine, are also an ideal choice. Others that normally climb but will also trail and soften include ivy-leaved pelargoniums and honeysuckle (*Lonicera*).

For smaller walls, a spreading plant that just oozes over the edge can be sufficient, such as a blanket of snow-in-summer (*Cerastium tomentosum*). Leave spaces for any required seating.

Tall-stemmed plants with fluffy flowers, such as *Dianthus*, soften a stone wall as well as provide gorgeous colour.

Stepping stone paths are an ideal compromise to achieve the functionality of a path without its bulk and formality. Planting groundcovers between and around the stepping stones, allows the path to be integrated into the garden, making it a less dominant feature. Choose flat-growing plants such as *Ajuga*, baby's tears (*Soleirolia*), *Pratia*, snow-in-summer or Australian native violet (*Viola hederacea*), or fragrant groundcover herbs that release their scent when stepped upon.

There are so many plants that can be utilized to soften edges, and these will vary considerably depending on the climate and soils where you garden. Some examples of small, strappy-leafed plants to provide a tufting texture for edging include mondo grass, the many *Liriope* cultivars, grasses such as *Carex* species and blue fescue (*Festuca glauca*), agapanthus either full-sized or dwarf cultivars, society garlic (*Tulbaghia*) and autumn crocus (*Zephyranthes candida*).

For flowering plants some of the many choices include seaside daisy (*Erigeron*), Serbian bellflower (*Campanula poscharskyana*), thrift (*Armeria*), pinks (*Dianthus*), rock cress (*Arabis*), geraniums and many members of the daisy family such as *Gazania*, *Arctotis*, *Dimorphotheca* and *Felicia*. Many

Edging a path can make it more formal or casual, depending on the species. Clockwise from top left: Mondo grass produces a wonderful fringing effect; the ice plant (*Lampranthus*) provides a bed of vivid colour for tall conifers; a mix of alyssum and violas soften the edges of a lawn; and seaside daisies spill gently onto a path.

annuals also make pretty borders, such as sweet Alice (*Alyssum*), pansies, petunias, lobelia and forget-me-nots.

Another dimension is added with the use of fragrant plants, particularly those with scented foliage. Use groundcover herbs such as chamomile, pennyroyal, oregano and the many varieties of thyme next to stepping stones and pathways where the fragrance of their crushed leaves will follow your footsteps. Next to pathways, taller plants with fragrant leaves include pelargoniums, lavender, lemon balm, *Santolina*, sage and other salvias and rosemary.

When selecting the right plants for the job, the amount of sun and shade is critically important. Some plants demand full sun and won't grow or flower without it, others need shade to protect their leaves from burning. When lining both sides of a path, or circling a lawn with an edging of the same plant, you may need an adaptable plant such as liriope that can cope in full sun through to shade.

Succulents make attractive edging along a pebbled pathway. These easy-care plants are particularly useful in dry climates.

PRUNING NOTES

Pruning is a lot simpler than many people think. If you use a little common sense and follow a few guidelines, you should get a good result every time.

WHEN TO PRUNE

The main point of pruning is to keep plants to the shape or size we want, or to make them bushier or bear more flowers and fruit. Although each plant has its own requirements and some types of pruning are specialized, for the most part, you can be guided by some general principles. The common-sense factor says that if you look at a plant and think that it needs pruning, then it probably does. Light pruning each year tends to be better than allowing a plant to grow unchecked for years and then having to cut into it heavily. If you are unsure about when to prune, a good rule of thumb is to prune immediately after flowering. Avoid pruning frost-tender plants until after the risk of frosts has passed in early spring, and don't prune in very hot weather.

SPECIFICS

Most of the plants featured in this book do not need a lot of pruning. Plants that are grown for their interesting or dramatic form usually develop that form without any interference from us. All that is needed is a bit of housekeeping—some tidying and clearing away—to ensure the plants are looking their best. Remove any dead leaves and those that are dying, diseased or discoloured, using secateurs to cut the leaf bases rather than pulling at them. Spent flower heads can also be removed (unless you want the seeds); this is known as deadheading. If they are on a long flower stalk, cut off the whole stalk as low down as possible. In some species, like a few of the rosette-forming succulents and bromeliads, the entire plant dies after flowering but is quickly succeeded by new 'pups' surrounding it. Simply clear away the whole dead plant.

Plants grown for their lush and coloured foliage, and those that form strappy clumps also tend to need little pruning. Palms and cordylines, for instance, are well known as low-maintenance plants and only ever need tidying. The shrubbier plants, such as acalypha and aucuba, can be lightly pruned to shape, but Hawaiian hibiscus will benefit from regular spring pruning to increase its bushiness and the number of flowers.

The groundcover plants that are featured in the Carpets chapter generally don't need pruning at all, except where they exceed their bounds. Use hedging shears to lightly contain their spread, or simply dig out unwanted sections of spreading plants such as thyme and native violet.

Plants featured in the chapter on Shapes and Hedges are the exception in this book, as these are shrubby plants chosen for their bushy habit and their ability to be pruned into particular shapes. Notes on pruning and training are included in the special section on Topiary, but the general rules still apply. Clip them lightly and frequently for best results when they are actively growing, unless they are forming flower buds.

TOOL CARE

Always buy good-quality pruning tools such as secateurs, hedging shears and loppers. Look after them and they will last for years. Clean off sticky sap after each use, and dry them to prevent rust forming. Sharpen your pruning tools regularly and never allow the cutting blades to contact soil as this will blunt them.

GLOSSARY

ACID SOIL: soil that has a pH of less than 7.

ALKALINE SOIL: soil that has a pH of greater than 7.

ANNUAL: a plant that has a natural lifecycle of one growing season, usually within a year.

AXIL: the part of the plant where the leaf joins the stem.

BIENNIAL: a plant that has a natural lifecycle of two years.

BRACT: a modified leaf attached to a flower or cluster of flowers; sometimes brightly coloured.

COMPOUND LEAF: any leaf that is made up of two or more leaflets.

CORM: an underground part of the plant used for food storage, and from which roots and leaves emerge.

CROWN: the top of the tree formed by the canopy; also the part of the plant where new shoots arise.

CULTIVAR: a distinct form of plant that has different features from the species; usually a result of selected breeding or cultivation.

CUTTING: a section of leaf, stem or root that is separated from a plant in order to reproduce it.

DEADHEADING: the removal of finished flowers in order to prevent seeds from forming; deadheading also encourages the production of new blooms.

DECIDUOUS PLANT: a plant that loses its leaves annually as part of its natural lifecycle.

DIVISION: a method of propagation by dividing a plant clump into smaller sections.

DOUBLE FLOWER: a flower that has more petals than the usual number in the species.

EVERGREEN: a plant that retains its leaves throughout the year.

FAMILY: a group of related plants; this includes genera and species.

FROND: the large compound leaf of a fern, palm or cycad.

GENUS: closely related plants, within a family, that share many characteristics; includes species.

HABIT: the plant's usual form, appearance and way of growing.

HYBRID: a plant which is the result of crossing different genera, species or cultivars.

INFLORESCENCE: a flowering stem of more than one flower.

NODE: the part of a stem from which the leaf or bud grows.

PANICLE: a branched flower cluster.

PERENNIAL: a plant that lives for more than two years; in gardens, the term mostly applies to non-woody plants, but can also describe the habits of shrubs and trees.

RHIZOME: a plant part used for food storage; may be underground or above ground; is usually horizontal.

SPECIES: very closely related plants, within a genus; the basic unit of classification.

TUBER: an underground part of the plant used for food storage, derived from a root or stem.

VARIETY: a particular type of a plant that has different features to the species but occurs naturally.

VARIEGATED: irregular colouring; a leaf or petal that is naturally green but displays other colours.

WHORL: a circular arrangement of three or more leaves or flowers arising from a single point on the stem.

PHOTO CREDITS

DELL ADAMS: 397.

JOE FILSHIE: 2, 4, 35, 51 bottom, 53, 68, 76–77, 82 top L, 87, 204–5, 212 top and bottom, 214, 233–234, 264 bottom L, 293, 298, 300 top, 301, 310, 330 bottom, 349, 389, 421, 436 top, 440 top and bottom, 454, 468 top R, 472 top R and bottom R, 474–5, 477, 478 top L and bottom R, 489.

DENISE GREIG: 191 bottom, 256, 326 bottom, 374.

TERRY MORRISSEY (ORCHID IMAGES, AUST): 316 bottom.

MURDOCH BOOKS PHOTO LIBRARY: Back cover (top left and bottom right), 61, 69–70, 71 top and bottom, 75, 82 top R, 88 bottom R, 92–3, 101, 103, 109 bottom, 115, 116 top and bottom, 120 top, 122, 123 top, 129, 139, 152, 161 top and bottom, 169, 178 bottom, 194 top L, 216 top, 219 top, 220, 231, 261, 274–5, 285, 287 top, 288, 294, 297 bottom, 319, 334 L, 336, 337 bottom, 342 top, 344, 345 bottom, 358 top R and bottom L, 402 top, 408 bottom L, 424 top, 425, 438, 441, 442 top, 445 bottom, 446 bottom, 448, 450–452, 455 top, 460 top, 464 centre, 468 top L, 472 top L, 481.

LORNA ROSE: Front cover, back cover (top centre, top right, bottom right), 6–8, 11–12, 14–5, 16, 19, 20, 22–3, 25–26, 29–34, 36–50, 51 top, 52 top and bottom, 55 top and bottom, 56, 57 top and bottom, 58–60, 63–67, 72–3, 74 top and bottom, 78 top and bottom, 79, 81, 82 bottom L and R, 84–5, 88 (top L and R, bottom L), 91, 94–100, 102 top and bottom, 104–109 top, 110–4, 117–118, 119 top and bottom, 120 bottom, 121, 123 centre and bottom, 124–125, 127, 130 (top L and R, bottom L and R), 135, 140–1, 142–3, 144–151, 153–7, 159–60, 162–5, 166 top and bottom, 167–168, 170–77, 178 top, 179–81, 183–184, 185 top and bottom, 186–187, 188 top and bottom, 189–190, 191 top, 193, 194 (top R, bottom L and R), 196–7, 199, 200 (top L and R, bottom L and R),

203, 206–15, 216 bottom, 217–218, 219 bottom, 222 bottom, 223–5, 226 top and bottom, 227, 230, 232, 235 L and R, 236 top and bottom, 237–238, 239 top and bottom, 240–6, 247 top and bottom, 248, 250–260, 263, 264 (top L and R, bottom R), 267, 268 (top L and R, bottom L and R), 271–3, 276–9, 280 top and bottom, 281–3, 284 top and bottom, 286, 287 bottom, 289–292, 296, 297 top, 299, 300 bottom, 302, 303 L and R, 304 L and R, 305, 306 top and bottom, 307–315, 316 top, 317–18, 320–3, 326 top, 327–8, 329 top and bottom, 330 top, 331–3, 334 R, 335, 337 top, 338–41, 342 bottom, 343, 345 top L and R, 346, 347 top and bottom, 348 (top L and R, bottom), 351, 352 (top L and R, bottom L and R), 354–5, 357, 358 top L and bottom R, 361, 362–8, 370–2, 375–386, 387 top and bottom, 388 top and bottom, 390, 391 (L, centre, R), 392, 395–396, 398 top and bottom, 399–401, 402 bottom, 403, 404 top and bottom, 405, 408 top L and bottom R, 411, 412 (top L and R, bottom L and R), 415–420, 422–3, 424 bottom, 426, 427 top and bottom, 428 top and bottom, 429, 431 top L and R, 432, 434–435, 436 bottom, 437, 439, 442 bottom, 443–444, 446 top, 447, 449 top and bottom, 453 L and R, 455 bottom, 456 top, 457–59, 460 bottom, 461–3, 464 top and bottom, 465–7, 468 bottom, 469, 471, 472 bottom L, 478 top R and bottom L, 482–3, 490.

DORA SCOTT: 373, 456 bottom

SUE STUBBS: 126, 131–2, 136 (top L and R, bottom L and R), 158 top and bottom, 182, 221, 222 top, 228, 229 top and bottom, 322, 324, 325 L and R, 407, 408 top R, 430, 431 bottom, 433, 445 top, 484, 487, 493–494.

PAT TAYLOR: 393

THE PUBLISHER WOULD LIKE TO ACKNOWLEDGE PHOTOGRAPHY IN THE FOLLOWING GARDENS. AUSTRALIA: Alstonville Tropical Fruit Research Station; Arcadia Lily Ponds Nursery; Arizona Cactus Garden; Ashcombe Maze; Austral Watergardens; Bay Street Nursery; Balmoral; Barmedman; Bay Cottage; Bebeah; Bonnie Banks; A Boxsell & K Smith; P & J Boyd; A Brescia; Bronte House; D Burke; Buskers End; N Butcher; Mr & Mrs Byrnes; Calthorpes House; Mr & Mrs Cannon; Carroll Creek Cottage; Bernard Chapman; Creek Cottage; Cockington Green; Convent Gallery;

E Cossil & T Carlstrom; Chinese Gardens; Cloudehill; Cooramilla Nursery; Margaret Cory Garden; B Cottee; Craigie Lea; Cranebrook Native Nursery; Dr G Cummins; Darwin Botanic Gardens; G & D Davey; Davidson's Wholesale Nurseries; Djanbung Gardens; Dunedin; Dunrath; K & P Edwards; Eryldene; Eudlo Cycad Gardens; Eurondella; Mr & Mrs Evans; Fairyburn; Johnniefields; A Ferguson; Fernbrook Gardens; Finches of Beechworth; Field's Cacti & Succulents Garden; Fletcher Botanic Gardens; Forest Edge; Lillian Fraser Garden; Galapagos Farm; Gardenworld; Mr & Mrs Geekie, Gemas; M Glasson; B Goleby; Gowan Brae; Mr & Mrs Greene; Greenlaw; C & D Gribble; Mr & Mrs Haigh; J & J Hall; Hamilton's World of Cacti; J Hancock; M Hanks; M Hart; Mr & Mrs Heckenberg; Heronswood; D Hill; Hillview; K Hobbs; Howell Garden; Imperial Gardens; Mr & Mrs Ingram; Jaara Farm; R Johnstone; Kennerton Green; A & C Kent; Kings Park & Botanic Gardens; Klerk's Nursery; M Kirton; M & S Kvauka; Lambruk; Lavender Farm; Lawrence's Nursery; Lindfield Park; R & W Love; E Luke; F & J Lyons; R Machin; B Maloney; Medlow Bath; Menzies Nursery; Merry Garth; Miss Traill's House; Garden; R Mitchell; Moidart; H Moody; S Montgomery; A Morgan; P & B Mortlock; Mt Tomah Botanic Gardens; Nooroo; G & R Norris; P O'Malley; E Ommaney, Ross Garden Designs; Mrs Orpwood; A O'Sullivan; Out of Town Nursery; Palmland Nursery; Paradise Palms Golf Club; Mr & Mrs Park; Parkers Nursery; Pine Crest; Plassy; Pockets; Red Cow Farm; G & G Rembel; D & F Rex; Rippon Lea; Royal Botanic Gardens, Melbourne; Royal Botanic Gardens, Sydney; Royal Tasmanian Botanical Gardens; Rose Cottage; J Ross; J & L Rowan; B Rymer; J & P Sargent; D Scott; M Shepherd; Shirley; Silky Oaks Lodge; H Skountzos; D Smith; J Stowar; S Swain; Swane's Nursery; Tambourine Mountain Garden Centre; Pat Taylor; Terragram; The Bromeliad Man; The Flax Man; The Folly; The Fragrant Garden; The Iveys; The Olive Branch; The Parterre Garden; The Wildflower Farm; Ann Thomson Garden Advisory Service; D & B Thompson; Tamar House; A & R Tonkin; Jan Waddington's Nursery; Wagga Wagga Botanic Gardens, Welby Garden Centre; Weerona; Mr & Mrs Westaway; A Wilkes; D Williamson; S Wilson; Wollongong Botanic Gardens; Wombat Hill Estate; Yengo; A Ziller. NEW ZEALAND: Brown Sugar Café; Gethsemane; Kevin Kilsby Ceramics; Lyddington Garden; B McConnell; R & G Muir; Titoki Point, Tregamere; Woodleigh Farm Garden; P Zino. UK: Royal Botanic Gardens, London.

INDEX

Murdoch Books® Australia
Pier 8/9, 23 Hickson Road,
Millers Point NSW 2000
Phone: + 61 (0) 2 4352 7000
Fax: + 61 (0) 2 4352 7026

Murdoch Books UK Limited
Erico House, 6th Floor North,
93/99 Upper Richmond Road, Putney
London SW15 2TG
Phone: + 44 (0) 20 8785 5995
Fax: + 44 (0) 20 8785 5985

Published in 2003 by Murdoch Books®, a division of Murdoch Magazines Pty Ltd.
©Text, design, and photographs copyright Murdoch Books® 2003

Printed by Midas Printing (Asia) Ltd
PRINTED IN CHINA

National Library of Australia Cataloguing-in-Publication Data.
Stackhouse, Jennifer. Form & foliage guide to planting.
Includes index. ISBN 1 74045 375 1 1. Foliage plants.
2. Landscape gardening. I. Young, Helen, 1958-. II. Title. 635.975

Chief Executive: Juliet Rogers
Publisher: Kay Scarlett

Editor: Carla Holt
Design: Alex Frampton
Design Concept: Marylouise Brammer
Creative Director: Marylouise Brammer
Editorial Director: Diana Hill
Production: Monika Paratore